BUILDING YOUR MOVEABLE
TINY HOUSE WITH
MINDFULNESS

WRITTEN BY
PATRICK SUGHRUE

Move·a·ble ti·ny house:
A house for year round living
that's less than 400 square feet
and built on a trailer.

Mind·ful·ness:
The state of active, open atten-
tion to the present. When you're
mindful, you carefully observe
your thoughts and feelings without
judging them good or bad. Instead
of letting your life pass you by,
mindfulness means living in
the moment and awakening to
your current experience, rather
than dwelling on the past or
anticipating the future.

INTRODUCTION

I have several goals in mind for writing this book. One of the primary ones is to teach the creative process.

I have been so amazed by the power we have as humans to 'create' that I've devoted much of my adult life to helping folks design and then build their dream homes. I'm now at a place in my life where I want to use a Tiny House on Wheels (THoW) to teach others the wonder of this creative process. The mechanics of the process are actually very simple. Stepping through them is where life, growth and maturity flourish. The creative process works for things as simple as making a loaf of bread or building a new raised bed in your garden. With the creation of your own home, the scope just gets larger.

"Happiness is achieved when you stop waiting
for your life to begin and start making
the most of the moment you are in."

- Germany Kent

Published in Vancouver, Washington
United States of America by Artisan Tiny House llc.

Library of Congress Cataloging-in-Publication Data

Sughrue, Patrick, 1950-
  Building Your Moveable Tiny House with Mindfulness

  ISBN 978-1-7322067-0-0 Tradepaper
  ISBN 978-1-7322067-1-7 ePub
  ISBN 978-1-7322067-2-4 PDF

  1. Tiny House on Wheels. 2. Mindfulness. 3. Structural Insulated Panels.
  4. Building Workbook. 5. Tiny House on Wheels. 6. Moveable Tiny Homes.

DISCLAIMER:
The contents of this book are provided for informational purposes only and should not be construed as advice. While all information shared here is believed to be accurate, the author of this book specifically disclaims all warranties - expressed, implied or statutory - regarding the accuracy, timeliness, and/or completeness of the information contained herein. Please discuss any specific needs with a qualified professional.

Acknowledgments

Thanks to . . .

Jill Sughrue for editing and encouragement.

Sarah Susanka, author of <u>The Not So Big House</u> and <u>The Not So Big Life: Making Room for What Really Matters,</u> for her inspiration.

Things Align Design for branding and book design.

Clients who entrusted their dream homes into my hands.

All who have walked the creative path before and bring us to this point.

For Jill, my true companion

TABLE OF CONTENTS

CHAPTER ONE
Getting Ready for the Journey

GETTING READY FOR THE JOURNEY

"We become what we behold. We shape our tools,
and thereafter our tools shape us."
- Marshall McLuhan

The creative process is one of the most amazing opportunities we have as humans on this planet. I was always building things as I was growing up, but it wasn't until my early 20s that I really discovered the creative process for myself. I admired a friend's leather coat and thought to myself how much I'd really like one too (with apologies to my vegan friends). But I didn't have the money to buy one, so . . .

STEP 1
I began thinking about it; dreaming about it. Then I made a sketch or two.

STEP 2
I looked for a sewing pattern that with an adjustment or two would work for the coat I wanted.

STEP 3
I bought a piece of leather and since I had a plan I was able to determine just how much I needed so I wouldn't have a lot of wasted scraps.

STEP 4
I cut it out and learned to sew leather by hand with an awl, cross-stitching through the seams. I hand-crafted buttons from the limb of a Yew tree in Neil Creek Canyon. As I was looking for a good hardwood to use, I also learned about some of the other trees that grew in the canyon. It's amazing what you might learn along the way to your intended goal.

STEP 5
Holding up the finished jacket, I relished in the realization that it was exactly what I had pictured in my mind! I'm not one to keep a lot of stuff, but I still have that jacket as a reminder of the powerful process of creation.

THE PRACTICE

MANIFEST IT

You will see it when you believe it. If you believe it, you will see it.

BE HERE NOW

The experience is in the journey, not the final goal. You will always have another something to build or another project to do. Enjoy this one by practicing being fully present along the way. No one is always present, but we can always be practicing.

KEEP IT SIMPLE

Break it down step by step and enjoy each one. Move from the simple to the complex. If you don't have a lot of experience, don't start with the most intricate details. *You wouldn't give a 3-year-old a 500-piece jigsaw puzzle.*

THE CREATIVE PROCESS

THE IDEA

Snap, crackle, pop! Pictures and ideas are racing through your mind. This is the inspiration. Your thoughts just keep coming back to it.

THE SHARE

You write it down, sketch it out, make a list, start a drawing, or build a model. You know you're in the flow when you just have to get *it*- whatever *it* is - out of your head and into the world.

People proceed with this part of the process differently, depending on which discipline you are working in. For centuries the building industry has used certain conventions for clarifying and sharing an idea with others on the team. The most common way is with a floor plan: a view from above showing dimensions for the width and length of the building, dividing the space into areas, and placing symbols for objects like appliances, cabinets and furniture in them.

But keep in mind that this view does not give us any information on heights. For that you need 'elevations' that are shown on the outside of the building and in sections through the building (e.g. the loft is 6'-4" above the floor). Once you have a legible plan that can be read and understood by others, you can move to the next step. Lots of folks are having success using Sketchup, a free 3D drawing program from Google. What you can do with the free version is amazing. At some point you will need to print out views from your 3D model. At the very least you will need the floor plan, all four elevations, and sections through both directions, with dimensions.

THE MATERIALS

In the construction industry it is common to use a tool called a take-off form, where you determine what and then how much of any materials you will need. For example, how many shingles, or how much siding will it take for each side of the building? How many windows do you need, and what are their sizes and locations? This can be a very fun part of the process if you think of it as a puzzle with a scavenger hunt thrown in. Download an example at Bonus Material link.

THE PERSPIRATION

Now we start the build, the hard physical work. This can be fun or grueling depending on your attitude. Pace yourself, this is not a sprint. A little done every day is better than stop and go.

THE REVEAL

The thing that was only an idea in your head is now a reality!

Once you learn to trust the process, you'll
find yourself recognizing it and using it
in every area of your life.

YOU SAY YOU WANT TO BUILD IT

At some point you must commit to the project. Then the challenge is to stay engaged. What I mean by 'engaged' is always thinking about the steps in front of you; researching the best ways to proceed. Read articles in publications like the Journal of Light Construction or Fine Home Building. This is your build! You are the general contractor. It is up to you to set the standard. If you are building with a partner, sit down and talk about who will take the lead on which parts, and how to resolve an impasse in the hundreds of decisions you will need to make. After all the research is done, someone has to say, "Let's do it this way." Then let it go. There is no "perfect" tiny house. If you are not the cook, then stay out of the kitchen. What I mean is let the person who does most of the cooking design that part.

In most cases, this will be your first major construction project; even if you've done remodeling projects or built a house before, keep in mind that nothing is perfect. You are building a square box on a round planet. If you don't get it right on this one you can do it on the next one. Just remember building a tiny house is a little like bringing a baby into the world, you might want to give yourself and your partner a little time before you start talking about the next one.

There will also come a point along the journey where you'll say to yourself: why in the world did I start this project? What was I thinking? When you do, it's important to remember that you are not the first person to come to that point; you are in good company. It is part of the hero's journey. Do not despair. Take a break if you need to. Ask for more help to get over that hump.

If you persevere you will also reach that day where you will say: WOW, I did it! I built my own home. I can do anything! I am the queen/king of the universe!

WHAT'S DRIVING YOUR PROJECT?

By driver I mean the thing that propels you forward: the fervor, zeal, passion, enthusiasm....

Why _are_ you building a Tiny House on Wheels?

It could be for one or more of several reasons. Are you looking to have a smaller footprint? Do you want to enjoy life more? Is it to reduce your cash out-flow so you can do work you really love?

My drivers are simplicity, durability, energy-efficiency and ease of construction. Here are some that others have mentioned:

- Freedom from rent or mortage
- Mobility
- Least cost
- Cool looking
- Totally Automated
- Off-the-Grid

It's important to identify your drivers early on in the process so when you get tired you can look back and remember where you're going and why you want to go there. Things constantly change. People fall in love and hookup; people fall out of love and separate. Babies are born and people die. Go with the flow; it is all good and all part of life. It only hurts when we hang on too tightly. So take some time here to identify your drivers. Seriously use the space in the DESIGN section of Chapter 2 to do some brainstorming and define three or four primary drivers for yourself or with your partner if you are building together. This is the right time to decide if you can agree on the purpose for starting this build, not half way through the project.

Turn your attention for a moment to 'the system.' I'm talking here about banking, mortgages, education, government, corporate America, investments, the industrial war complex, interstate highways, insurance, and even building zones and code systems.

Younger generations are already beginning to think of the system as the Dark Side (e.g. think _Star Wars_ or the unobtainium-seekers destroying everything in the process in _Avatar_).

Our modern day system tells us that a college education is the path to a good income and personal fulfillment. Many career paths are even blocked unless you play along. I'm not anti-education; just be aware that the education system may not be able to provide everything that's been promised. In many ways it's just another marketing machine selling a product and a service, not unlike a fancy pair of jeans. Many people in the THoW movement followed the system only to find that there was no job at the end of the degree that could meet their basic income needs, let alone provide enough excess to repay the (unforgivably high) student loans.

Then the system says "No worries; we have more for you. Just sign here and we'll sell you a $300,000 home and you can pay it off over 30 years, while you work at that job that sucks the joy out of you." And never mind that the banking system will extract $280,000 in interest from you while you pay it off. This is where many of the people I've worked with on a tiny house have said:

> *"Enough! I'm getting off the treadmill. I can build*
> *my own home for $30,000 to $50,000 and pay it off*
> *in three or four years instead of 30."*

Everyone who reads this will be in a different place as to how much they want to interface with the system. As a maturing hippie my preference would be to have as little to do with it as possible. That said, the reality for me, for now, is that I choose to use a local bank. I use the roads. I have a business so I need to register with the state. I touch the system where I have to, but try not to get enmeshed in it.

Where this pertains to some movable Tiny House builders is in deciding whether or not to follow a building code. The industry as a whole is rapidly moving toward using such a building code to guide the construction of Tiny Houses (see CODES in Chapter Two).

Now is also a good time to determine whether you will use financing of some kind and/or if you will insure or self-insure your new Tiny House on Wheels (THoW).

Don't box yourself in with deadlines if you don't need to. Projects of this size and magnitude take on a life of their own. Enjoy the process. Go with the flow.

The John Wayne era is over (i.e. "I can do this all by myself."). Work with a team; let others help. People are hungry for ways to come together in building community. You are robbing your friends and family of that opportunity if you don't allow them to help if they want to. Find appropriate ways for them to do so and provide the necessary guidance. When letting others help, you do need to provide clear instructions and share your expectations for the outcome.

The system will never provide for me more or less.

I am complete, whole and perfect right now.

Breathe in deeply, exhale ... I AM.

Resources:

Be Here Now by Ram Dass

The Power of Now by Eckhart Tolle

The Seat of the Soul by Gary Zukav

The Practicing Mind by Thomas Sterner

PLANNING

"Well begun is half done."
- Aristotle

The way I first heard it was from an old guy in Odell, Oregon, who said "A job well planned is a job half done." Seriously, this is the place to spend some time. Do you have what it takes to plan and then build your own home?

It's not just whether you have enough chutzpah: do you have enough money, enough time, a location? Do you have the necessary skills? If not, are you willing to dig in and acquire them?

The information is available everywhere, just be selective and aware that on YouTube there are plenty of people who really don't know what they are talking about and are happy to document it. To those who enjoyed the education system, think of your Tiny House build as a master's degree program. It costs about the same and could take about the same amount of time to complete.

On the plus side, not only will you end up with more than a certificate to hang on the wall, you will have completed your own home. Should you change your mind about living in it later, you can even get your money back by selling it or renting it out for years of income.

If you want to learn the right way to do a certain aspect of your building project, I recommend two sources:

Journal of Light Construction:
I have been a reader of this magazine for about twenty years and I still learn or relearn something every month. I highly recommend joining the online service to access all of their content. There is also a users' group where you can ask questions about any of the articles. I like the printed JLC field guides, drawings and charts.

<u>Fine Home Building:</u>
I have read this Taunton Press publication over the past years to stay current in my field of residential construction. You will also find a host of online information and resources.

To subscribe to both publications costs about $80 a year. To have most current professional information on any task you are undertaking literally at your fingertips is a VERY SMALL price.

There are various ways to accomplish a task: good, better and best. Best will always take a little longer and usually costs a little more in materials. Best practice is what this is called in the building trades. I'll let you decide which level you want to build to.

I have found that real craftsmen
are usually happy to share their knowledge
with anyone willing to ask.

Resources:
<u>Tiny House Magazine.com</u>
<u>Tiny House Design.com</u>

CONSTRAINTS

"Creativity comes from constraint."
- Biz Stone

By constraints in our context I mean the parameters within which you will need to build your THoW. You know, the proverbial box: how high, how wide, and how heavy?

Since we also live on a planet that exerts loads (e.g. stresses, forces, etc.) on a building, if you want all of your hard work last more than a few years you will need to take these forces and other considerations into account.

HEIGHT	Standard	13'-6" (Remember those tunnels on the road.)
WIDTH	Standard	8'-6" (You can build wider, but will need a permit to haul.)
LENGTH	Maximum	36' (Yes, it could probably be longer, but why?)
WEIGHT	Depends on	Gross Vehicle Weight (GVW) of your trailer.
CODE	Depends on	Which one you choose, if any. (I suggest Park Model.)
LOAD	Wind	70 mph (You should never tow faster than 60 mph.)
LOAD	Snow	25 lb. Minimum
DOLLARS	You only have __$ to spend.	
TIME	You have to be out of your apartment by _____.	
VEHICLE	You only have a ¾-ton truck to haul it.	

Of course you can ignore any or all of these, but that will present challenges later.

Resources: Tiny House Magazine.com   Tiny House Design.com

CODES

"Codes are a puzzle. A game, just like any other game."
- Alan Turing

> ### ANSI A119.5
> ### Park Model
> ### Recreational Vehicle
> ### Standard
> ### 2015 Edition

If you want to play the game, here is what you need to know. First, understand that building codes are different than, but related to, zoning. Zoning tells you where you can place a building: RVs go in RV parks, Park Models go in Park Model parks, and houses go in places that are zoned for homes. See an example of zoning law (ordinance) in BONUS MATERIAL. Codes, by contrast, provide information about how a particular building is supposed to be constructed.

There are several National codes that could relate to your THoW construction. They were all written for either manufacturers or professional builders since, relatively speaking, few people build their own homes. For this reason, you might find these codes difficult to understand and even harder to implement, especially when you don't work with them every day or don't agree with them.

This is a good place to practice breathing and letting go; it won't do you any good to get upset or angry. As a society we have created this system of codes for living in harmony with our neighbors. It is what it is. The only decision to make now is whether to play or not to play; then be willing to accept the consequences of your decision.

THE CODES TO CONSIDER WHEN THINKING OF A THoW

There is a code for manufacturers of Recreational Vehicles (RVs): ANSI 119.0. This is the code that RVIA, a trade organization, uses for RVs like pop-up tents, travel trailers, and motor homes.

There is a code for manufacturers of Park Models, which are more like manufactured homes than RVs due to their size, construction with more durable building materials, and higher R-values. Unfortunately, they are still assigned to the RV world: ANSI A119.5 (available online from RVIA).

There is a code for Manufactured Homes known as the HUD-code and administered by the U.S. Department of Housing and Urban Development.

There is another code for homes or modular buildings built on a foundation, which is the International Residential Code (IRC). States can adopt this code 'as is' or make changes to it (e.g. both Oregon and Washington have strengthened the energy-efficiency sections). While the IRC is updated every year, states may lag in implementing the changes. Oregon is currently using the 2014 version and Washington is using the 2015 version as we go to print. All of these codes are intended for manufacturers or contractors that build units for others. The underlying motive for all of these codes is to protect life, health and safety, as well as providing the next owner with confidence that it was built to a certain level of professionalism.

For our purposes, there are three distinct issues that need to be addressed: 1) Which code should moveable Tiny Houses be built to or do we need a new one? 2) Who should verify/certify that the work is completed to the code? 3) Where can you park one to live in it year round?

When I built my first tiny house on wheels in 1973 no one worried about codes as it was all done under the radar. Today there are 114-million more people in the USA and a much more complex society. With a plethora of television shows devoted to the subject, the tiny house movement has exploded into the American culture adding impetus to the demand to build this 'new type' of home to Code.

During my years of designing Tiny Houses on Wheels, I have concurred with the opinion of the Washington Department of Labor and Industries (the agency that oversees RV, Park Model and manufactured building codes in Washington state) that the Park Model (PMRV) code is the most appropriate one to use for THoWs. Park Models are built with more durable materials than RVs since RVs are designed to be as light as possible and only used for temporary, recreational occupancy (e.g. in the summer months).

Under the current Park Model code, the minimum required insulation values are R-5 in the floor and walls, and R-7 for the roof – not very much at all. I believe this is one of the main reasons RVs, including Park Models, are limited to seasonal use. By significantly upgrading the insulation and making a few other improvements, I think it is feasible to live in a THoW year round. Time will tell if the powers that be will agree with me.

No matter which code you are talking about, remember that they are all MINIMUM codes. You can always build better; there is no law against that.

TO CERTIFY OR NOT TO CERTIFY, THAT IS THE QUESTION

In the world of IRC ground-bound houses, the local building jurisdiction sends out a building inspector at various stages during the course of construction to make sure you are doing things right (i.e. it is being built according to the approved set of plans).

The same thing holds true for most manufacturers of RVs and Park Models. They hire a third party inspection service to come by from time to time to observe and, if satisfied, issue a report saying the construction is being done properly and thereby extend the certification.

For a single builder like yourself, there are currently two different companies I know of that are willing to provide a similar service. They are Bildsworth International and Pacific West Associates Inc.

Whether or not you choose to use either of these services, I strongly suggest you start a 3-ring binder and include the following:

- **Printed materials:** that come from the manufacturer for everything you purchase - from the trailer itself to the kitchen faucet.

- **Photos:** yes, actual hard copy photos or pictures printed on 8.5 x 11 paper. You can still get them printed at places like Walgreens and Costco. Take a picture of your trailer and the floor construction and how it attaches to the trailer. Include photos of the framing or panel assembly showing the SIP screws in the corners and those holding down the roof.

- **Worksheets:** showing calculations for the loft, stairs, etc.

- **Receipts:** especially ones that show you bought a higher grade of lumber for the loft.

- **Appliance manuals**

- **Labels:** from paints and finishes.

This will become the owner's manual for your home. In the midst of the build it is easy to forget to keep this current, but it will pay big dividends later. An owner's manual is a requirement of the Park Model code.

At the very least, acquire a binder and a box big enough for it to fit in. You can throw all the documents that will someday go into a binder into it. At the very least it will keep everything in one place until you make time on a rainy day to put it together.

This discussion about codes and inspections will no doubt continue for many years. My advice at this time is to build to the PMRV code and have it certified by a third party company like Bildsworth or Pacific West. Once again, document everything you do with labels, receipts and photos.

Okay, now that you know what you're getting into,
let's move on to the next step.

Resources:
Tiny Houses on Wheels and the Affordable Housing Crisis

COUNTING THE COSTS

*"Everything comes with a price. Everything.
Some things just cost more."*

- Brom

People ask me all the time: How much does it cost to build a Tiny House on Wheels? My answer is always the same: *it depends*.

It's a great question and hopefully leads to the development of a good answer before going too much further. It's no fun getting part way through a project and suddenly finding that you really don't have enough money, time or even energy to follow it through to the finish.

It costs more than you may think to build a safe, energy efficient, and quality tiny home. I know we've all seen the internet stories of the tiny house built for under $2,000. Well, good luck with that. I'm not saying you can't find great deals on remnants, and reclaimed materials for incorporating into your home; I'm an avid Craigslist shopper myself. What I am saying is that, at a minimum, you should start with a safe and durable foundation for your home. The shell (i.e. floor, walls and roof) needs to be strong and secure enough to withstand all the forces that will be acting upon it (e.g. wind, snow, ice, freeway travel). The cost of the materials for those minimal standards will add up to thousands of dollars even for a modest 8'x16' model.

Another reason I say 'it depends' is because everyone's circumstances are unique. One person might need to rent a space to park their trailer while they build it out; the next person can do it in their back yard. Some people have a shop full of the necessary tools or perhaps an interested family member who does have the tools and wants to help. The next person needs to buy, rent and/or borrow the many tools it takes to complete their tiny home.

We all have different skill sets. Some people know how to use all the necessary tools or, if not, they are patient enough to take the time to learn. I'm the type of person who likes to learn new skills. I grab a book or watch three or four select YouTube videos and then I'm off to put my new knowledge to use, unafraid to make a mistake or two until I get it done right. Not everyone feels this way and that's okay. However, it does mean it will cost more to complete your home if you're not personally doing most of the work.

Aside from the trailer and exterior 'shell,' the interior finishes and fixtures can easily blow through any disciplined budget. There are some really cool items out there for outfitting tiny houses these days. This is an especially good place to practice 'being the observer.' Watch your emotions when you see that nifty stainless all-in-one sink unit or that awesome bookshelf that converts to a bed. It's a good time to check your list of drivers: does this item really meet my goals for living simply or debt-free or off-the-grid or ......?

In the home construction industry, a builder takes a new set of plans and starts from the ground up (i.e. the foundation) developing a spreadsheet of costs. He or she works up to the roofing, counting the cost for labor and materials for each different section along the way. If their crews don't do a particular job, let's say roofing or painting, they are sent out to subcontractors for bids.

When it comes to *your* tiny house, you are the builder and this is now your responsibility. You'll find a handy spreadsheet for estimating your costs in bonus material. I would encourage you to use it. Spreadsheets are a great tool. Have fun with it.

Regardless of your budget, you need to keep in mind that, like any project of this size, there will undoubtedly be changes along the road to completion. These changes can affect how long it will take to finish it and how much it will ultimately cost. Some sections will cost more and some could even cost less (not often but it can happen). That's okay, but without a budget to start with you won't know where you are and not knowing can add a lot of stress.

When you start looking at the cost of materials, hopefully you will notice that there is usually, but not always, a direct correlation between cost and quality. There are some places where quality counts and some places where it may not be as important. That said, this is where you need to recognize those fundamental components that can't be upgraded later. For example, a ¼" lag bolt costs less, but does not have the same holding power (quality) as a ½" through-bolt with a bearing plate when used to attach the floor to the trailer, and it can't be replaced later. On the other hand, entry door hardware prices can range significantly; maybe you could use lower cost hardware now and eventually buy the higher quality one you really want. It's also a good time to remain flexible and consider some trade-offs, like a higher quality item on Craigslist that isn't exactly the style you envisioned, but is a great deal. You will face the choice between quality and price many times throughout your build. Start by setting your priorities and sticking to your goals.

Just like with materials, if you hire someone to help with parts of your build, the cost and quality can very widely. Do your homework; ask for references. Spend enough time with anyone you are thinking of hiring to get a feel for his or her aptitude and attitude. The most important job for you when hiring someone is to communicate what you want them to do. In the construction industry this is done with a good set of specifications, document(s) outlining exactly what materials are to be used and to what level of expertise. This can be so detailed as to indicate how far apart fasteners are to placed, what length they will be, and even how thick the plating is to be on them. You won't need that level of detail here. I suggest writing down in plain language what you want, and have a copy for each of you to refer back to.

Bonus Material

FINANCING YOUR TINY HOUSE

"Every financial worry you want to banish and financial
dream you want to achieve comes from taking tiny steps
today that put you on a path toward your goals."

- Suzy Orman

If you can pay for your tiny house with cash, that's obviously the way to go. Maybe you have a nice savings account, or you got a buyout or a severance package. Sometimes the universe drops money in your lap. If so, use it wisely. It is okay to have money left in the bank when you are done.

Another way to pay for your THoW with cash is to build it in stages. Save up enough to buy the trailer. Then save up for the shell, door and windows; just be sure you have enough to cover it properly with a weather resistive barrier (WRB), also known as house wrap, and roof underlayment. Then save up and buy the siding and roofing. At some point you can move into your home to finish it up. You don't need an occupancy permit from some government agency for a THoW.

FINANCING

Not everyone who wants to build a THoW has $25,000 to $40,000 at their disposal. There are a couple of ways to finance your tiny home. Credit cards are the easy answer. The downside to charging everything is, of course, the interest rate and the temptation to keep on using it and getting off budget.

A home equity loan might be the answer if you are downsizing from an existing home. You could borrow the money needed to build your tiny home from the equity in your existing home, then pay it off when you sell the big house.

There are also a couple of institutions that will finance a THoW like they would an RV. Most of them are looking for a finished product, however, where a certified THoW is the norm. In the interim, you might be able to secure a 'bridge' loan from a family member or friend to finance the build and then convert it to an RV loan when it is finished.

Another option is to 'pay as you go.' I know this isn't very popular these days, but it still works. If you want it bad enough it will happen, though maybe not this month or even this year.

LightStream.com – Tiny Home/Park Model (financing for finished models)

TIME

"You can do anything, but not everything."

- Anonymous

The way I learned it was, "You can do anything you want in life, you just can't do it all at once." I say this here because I see some of my tiny house friends, who've done so many other things in life whenever they wanted, but just can't seem to figure out why this is taking so long.

Okay, you say you're in and want to build a THoW. How long is it going to take, you ask? Really, how long? As an older and wiser friend of mine used to say "Pat, what's your hurry?" Of course it took me years to understand that he wasn't really interested in my answer, he was telling me to slow down: there is no place to be, no place to go; it only seems like there is.

Yeah, yeah, but how long? .....Short answer: *it depends*.

Let's say you're retired, laid off or otherwise able to work on it full time AND have the funds to move forward at each step. Now add the help and availability of another person, where at least one of you knows what you are doing. Next assume you have all the tools and supplies that you'll need at your disposal. So far, so good. What's left, and is often overlooked, is all the time it takes to run around and fetch the stuff for the next step.

One tip for making the build go smoother is analogous to playing chess: you need to think two or three moves ahead. You should be acquiring the materials and preparing for the next step before you get there.

The point is there are too many variables to answer the 'how long' question definitely. See the day-by-day spreadsheet on the next page and add your best guess for the number of days it could take you. (Also available in Bonus Material.) You might easily add one more day per task just to get the materials lined up for the next step. And don't forget about birthday parties, storms, weddings, babies, and (sadly) even funerals.

ESTIMATED TIMELINE

TASK	TIME	YOUR ESTIMATE
Shell up (w/SIPs)	2 days	
WRB / Roofing Underlayment	2 days	
Windows and Door	2 days	
Roofing	2 days	
Siding and Trim	5 days	
Painting or Staining	1 day	
Exterior Total	12-14 days	
THE OUTSIDE IS FINISHED.		

TASK	TIME	YOUR ESTIMATE
Inside framing	2 days	
Plumbing - Rough in	2 days	
Electrical - Rough in	2 days	
Ceiling finish	1 day	
Wall finish	1 day	
Floor finish	1 day	
Cabinets and Counter	2 days	
Plumbing Finish	1 day	
Electrical Finish	1 day	
Trim Finish	1 day	
Interior Total	14-16 Days	
IT'S ALL FINISHED!		

A broad, more realistic time frame for Start-to-Finish could be from three months to one year; that seems to be the average.

Resources:
Getting Things Done by David Allen
Bonus Material

DESIGN DRIVERS

"Perfection is achieved, not when there is nothing more to add, but when there is nothing left to take away."
- Antoine de Saint Exupéry

What makes the best design?....*It depends.*

It depends on *your* goals and intention – your *design drivers*. It is important to define these early on in the process so you can refer back to them as you move through the project.

Your design drivers will affect the look, size, and layout of the floor plan of your THoW. Sometimes these can be reduced to an if/then decision process. For instance, if you want solar photovoltaic (PV) and/or rain collection, then the roof will most likely be a single plane – either side-to-side or front-to-back – in order to have the most surface area. Other considerations are often attributable to the way we have been imprinted; that is, I want what I want because it just feels right.

I'm a firm believer in scaling down your tiny house. That means making everything slightly smaller. Your windows should be smaller; the door narrower and maybe slightly shorter. This carries inside to the cabinets and countertops.

In designing THoWs for clients, some of the most fun I have is working with couples who come from different backgrounds with very specific individual ideas. What a great opportunity to learn the art of the compromise. Be sure to have fun with it!

Don't get too hung up in the details. It never ends up exactly like you planned, and that is okay. Go with the flow. Some of my best designs have actually come out of mistakes.

After several years of tiny house design and working with lots of people, I have found that the following sizes seem to work well for peaceful, long term habitation:

- For one person, a 16' long THoW is a minimum, but 20' might be better.

- For two smaller folks, 20' is a minimum, but 24' is more common.

- For a couple with a child, 28' or even 36' seems more reasonable.

If your building skills are minimal and your budget is limited, keep it simple and you will have a much better chance of finishing your home.

I know there are lots of really cool looking designs out there with bump-outs and pop-ups and super widgets and beds that go up and down. They also require larger budgets and skilled workers to build them. It is just fine to be where you are with your time and talents.

Here are some examples of Design Drivers that clients have shared with me:

- I want the most cubic feet of enclosed space that's possible.

- It needs to accommodate __ people.

- It needs to be the easiest to build.

- I want the lowest cost possible.

- It must have a loft.

- It must have a min. height of __" in the loft.

- It must have a min. height of __" under the loft.

- It must be one story with no loft.

- It must have a door on the _____ side.

- It must be built with SIPs.

- It must be built with steel studs.

- It needs a certain look: cabin, modern, southwest, _____.

- I want to be totally off the grid.

- I want solar PV on the roof.

- I need it to collect rainwater.

- I want to travel a lot with my THoW.

Take some time to think about **your** design drivers.

How does it look from THE OUTSIDE?

This is the place where lots of other folks usually start. Is it one-story or a story and a half with a loft? What is the shape of the roof? Is it flat or sloped to one side with a ridge in the middle like a cabin in the woods?

This is where you need to get out your list of drivers. If one of them is to travel to 49 states with your home, then a 36-foot 5th-wheel may not be the ticket. That driver will push you toward a 16-foot or maybe a 20-foot. It will likely have a sloped or curved roof from front to back. If I were to pull it, I would want it to be no more that 8 feet tall. On the other hand, if you know it is going to be settled on your own land, then go for the big one if that is what you want.

Here are some basic roof shapes:

FLAT: This gives you the most room inside in the loft; however, if it rains or snows a lot where you are this might not be the best shape.

SINGLE SLOPE - SIDE TO SIDE: might be bettter for those conditions. Keep in mind that different roffing materials have limits to how shallow the roof can be.

SINGLE SLOPE - CURVED FRONT TO BACK: gives less wind resistence when you are hauling it, so you get better mileage, thereby adding less carbon to the atmosphere.

GABLE ROOF: Looks the cutest (to many) and reminds me of our log cabin history. It is the hardest to build for a variety of reasons and creates point loads on your trailer. When you throw in a dormer with a different pitch, you have added another layer of complexity. Obviously it is not impossible to deal with these issues as there are plenty of gables out there. Just a thought when you are weighing all your options.

GABLE - FRONT TO BACK: is another shape I like. It can lessen the amount of wind you need to push and give you a nice loft in the back of your tiny home.

Bonus Material: Roof Styles

Now to the inside: The FLOOR PLAN.

When designing, I tell my clients there are really only two decisions to make at this stage: where the door goes and where the kitchen window is located. Unless you know exactly where every cabinet and piece of furniture will go, it will probably change. Most folks have a hard time seeing something that isn't there yet. If you know where you are going to park your home, go ahead and plan the view side windows. But remain flexible. I recently had a client swap the kitchen and bathroom end for end after it was built. That's okay.

There are lots of resources online for floor plans, so I'll let that one go. I would suggest you purchase three or four other books to get a larger perspective on your project. Even if you buy $100 worth of books and then decide this may not be for you after all, that is a small price to pay.

I'm not saying that these things are unimportant. Here's where you need to refer back to your drivers. Do you have a year to play with optional floor plans?

There are some major decisions that if made early on in your process will either eliminate or make other decisions easier:

>Do you know where you are going to park it? If yes, and it's possible, place it with the long side facing south since this always makes good sense in the northern hemisphere.

>Are you going to put PV panels on the roof now or later? If yes, then a side-to-side single slope roof would be best. (You can also put panels on a pole; they do not need to be on the roof.)

>Is it a smaller unit and you really plan to travel with it? If so, put the door on the left or in the back and that way you won't be stepping into the street whenever you go in and out.

Start your floor plan with a sheet of notebook or grid paper. Do your best to get the major decisions out of the way early on.

Start with the width. Most folks draw a thin line for the walls, but keep in mind that they are usually between 4-1/2" and 5" thick, so make it a thicker double line. (For example, an 8-foot wide THoW leaves you with about 7'-3" for an inside measurement.)The outside of the same ThoW will end up about 8'-2" wide after siding and trim. I design plans for up to an 8'-9" wide moveable tiny house in which case the interior measures 8'-0" and the outside about 9'-0". (It does require a permit to haul it, but no flaggers or signs.)

Next move on to the length. Some companies will build any length; however, I recommend working with even numbers to reduce lumber waste (e.g. 24 feet vs 25 feet). Again draw a thick double line for your walls or just a single line for whatever the inside dimension will be. Don't forget to draw in the fenders; for most homes they will protrude into the inside by 4-6 inches. It's easy to put in cabinets that go over them; not as easy to put a door or refrigerator there. The length of the fender itself varies by manufacturer, but with a two-axle trailer will be about six feet long and with a triple-axle about 8'-6" to 9' long. For most manufacturers, the center of the axles will be at roughly 60% of the length of the floor from the front (e.g. a 24' trailer will have the fender centered at about 14'5").

With regard to doors, I'm not a big fan of 6' sliders or French doors, because they weaken the wall, take up so much space, and are only R-2. You can also get lots of light from a 36" wide glass door and you have a lot more options as to where it can go.

Start with the majors and then move to the smaller details. Now that you have your fenders and door placed, pick a location for a 36" cabinet for the kitchen sink. It can help at this point to have small pieces of paper with the correct dimensions for furniture and counters, so you can move them around as you play with ideas.

Have fun. It's okay if you feel that you made

a mistake here and there. You can recover from

most of them with a good story to tell.

Bonus Material: Floor Plans

GREEN BUILDING

"The best time to plant a tree was 20 years ago.
The next best time is today."
- Chinese proverb

Green building is a defined set of parameters applied systematically to make a home not only healthier, but more durable and energy efficient. You'll find a few of the myriad resources about green building at the end of this section, so I won't take up much space here.

There are several green building programs across the country to help builders make wise choices in many areas of the construction process and many include a Certification process.

The various green building programs include many or all of the following components:

- Improving indoor air quality for the health and comfort of the occupants.
- Using water wisely to save money and conserve the water table.
- Increasing energy efficiency to reduce energy bills and lower your eco-footprint.
- Using durable materials that require minimal maintenance and replacement.
- Sourcing materials wisely and using resources efficiently.
- Buying materials locally to support your community.
- Using salvaged, reclaimed and/or recycled materials.
- Building smaller, more compact homes. We have this one down!

In short, green building is about thinking long term versus short term. It's not only about the initial cost of something, but takes into consideration the total cost of using, maintaining and ultimately disposing of something. Take the example of a washing machine. A front-loader may cost more than a top-loader, but if you add up the savings from using less detergent, less water and less energy over the life of that washer, let's say 20 years, it can easily add up to saving hundreds of dollars in the long run.

Green building is about taking care of the planet.

SAVING ENERGY SAVES EVERYTHING!

Resources:
Earth Advantage Institute
EPA – Green Building
NAHB – Intro to Green Building for Consumers
Green Builder Media

THE GREEN BUILDING PYRAMID

The goal for building green is to start with the easier things - at the bottom of the pyramid - and work your way up to the more complex and/or expensive items at the top. You will find house size at the bottom right. Okay, we've got this one.

The next level on the pyramid is about upgrading the envelope insulation and air sealing, and upgrading windows for better performance.

Next up you'll find an optimized water heater, low flow water fixtures and LED lighting.

Then is the push for Net Zero and adding solar panels.

One item builds on another until we create a sustainable world.

I encourage you to go to *www.greenbuildermedia.com* and check it out in more detail.

Thanks to Matt Power, Editor-In-Chief, Green Builder Magazine

BUILDING SCIENCE

"When we build, let us think that we build forever.
Let it not be for present delight nor for present use alone.
Let it be such work that our descendants will thank us for it."
- John Ruskin

Building science, according to Wikipedia, is the collection of scientific knowledge and experience that focuses on the analysis and control of the physical phenomena affecting buildings and architecture. In-other-words, how do the components of a building - together and separately - hold up under a variety of conditions (e.g. the elements, movement, etc.) and how can that knowledge be applied in the design of new techniques and technologies to enhance the life and performance of structures, including moveable Tiny Houses.

What I've learned from all the building science classes I've attended can be reduced to a few practical tips, ideas, or principles. First, it's known that buildings get ruined from water coming in from the outside and/or water condensation on the inside. We know how to address both of these challenges, but first it's necessary to acknowledge their existence and then we can take proper steps to mitigate the effects they have on a building. Mold and insects need three elements to thrive: food, warmth and moisture. Obviously there is plenty of 'food' in a THoW, like wood, paper and other organic matter. And since warmth is a given - we all like a comfy home - the one element we need to consciously control is moisture. If you keep your home below 55% relative humidity, there is little chance of a mold or insect problem caused by moisture.

Next, building science encourages us to build the BEST building we can under the given circumstances. I choose to think in terms of a 'high performance' building, which dictates four requirements.

HIGH PERFORMANCE BUILDINGS

1. AS MUCH INSULATION AS POSSIBLE. This equates to higher R-Values and lower U-values.

2. MINIMAL THERMAL BRIDGING. The usual 16" OC (on-center) framing is a lot of wood and at only R-4 per 2x4 makes a great bridge of thermal transfer.

3. RELATIVELY AIR TIGHT. The target here is 1 to 2 ACH (air changes per hour) at 50 pascals.

4. PROPERLY VENTILATED. This can be easily achieved with an 0.25 to 0.5 ACH exhaust fan or Energy Recovery Ventilator (ERV).

INSULATION

With a THoW you are limited to the amount of insulation simply by the thickness of the 2x4 wall. For this reason, it's wise to choose insulation with the highest R-value per inch. Yes, higher R-value does means higher cost, but now is the time to do things right. The likelihood of your walls being torn open later to upgrade or install better insulation is pretty slim. The beauty of insulation is that it has no moving parts, needs no service and, if properly installed or part of a SIPs wall, silently works for the life of the structure.

THERMAL BRIDGING

A thermal bridge is an area in a building envelope (e.g. a 2x4) which has a significantly higher heat transfer than the surrounding materials resulting in an overall reduction in thermal insulation of the building. What this means is that everywhere you put a stud or other solid piece of lumber that goes from the inside to the outside of the building, there is a 'bridge' of heat transfer and the R-value of the overall wall drops significantly.

AIR TIGHTNESS

This is simple. If you have excessive amount of cold or hot outside air blowing through your building, you will be uncomfortable and it will be harder and more expensive to heat or cool. I know there are still some folks who believe that buildings need to breathe, but I put them in the camp with climate change deniers. As the industry says: "Build it tight and ventilate it right!"

VENTILATION

Ventilation of an indoor space is how we deal with excess moisture. Did you know that, on average, a person exhales the equivalent of roughly 1.5 cups of water per day? Now think about the amount of water we use for bathing, cooking and watering our plants. Together these all make up the vapor load in your home and add up even quicker in a tiny house. By properly ventilating with an exhaust fan or ERV you can keep the relative humidity below that 55% level mentioned above. (Find a worksheet in the bonus material to figure out how much ventilation you need.)

Lastly, one of the best ideas to come out of the building science community is the application of a 'rainscreen' - a small space created between the sheathing of the structural wall and the siding. Unless you are planning to park your THoW in some remote and dry desert, it will be rained upon and the wind will blow against it. This small added space allows air to move between the siding and the sheathing of your building aiding in efficient moisture evaporation and removal. A rainscreen is a part of a building system. It can be accomplished by simply installing a building-wrap product like Hydrogap that provides a 1-mm space or by installing furring strips before applying the siding. The rainier the climate, the better the system you will need!

Resources:
Bonus Material (ventilation worksheet)
GreenBuildingAdvisor.com
Panasonic Fans
Rain Screen

INSURANCE

"Needing insurance is like needing a parachute – if it isn't there the first time, chances are you won't be needing it again."
- Anonymous

Insurance is definitely something you'll want to talk to an insurance agent about from both general liability and physical damage perspectives.

General liability insurance provides protection from a loss or lawsuit if a third-party (e.g. guest) is injured or becomes ill while in, on or around your home due to your 'negligence.' Traditional homeowners and renters liability coverage also extends to a situation where you accidentally injure someone even while you're away from your premises (e.g. at a friendly softball game where you're pitching).

Physical damage insurance covers the cost to repair or replace the building and/or contents up to a specified coverage limit subject to the deductible per loss.

You'll also want to be sure your THoW is covered during transport, possibly under your auto insurance policy, unless you want to take on that risk of loss yourself (i.e. no coverage would apply).

There are some insurance companies starting to offer coverage for THoWs.

Resources (at the time of printing):
InsureMyTinyHome.com ~ Portland, OR
Strategic Insurance Agency, LLC ~ Colorado Springs, CO 80906
Farmers Insurance ~ Portland, OR 97239 Adam Sinclair 971-254-1092

TOOLS

"Actions, good thoughts, and positive energy speak louder than judgmental words and are the most powerful tools you can use when working toward a better world."
- Madisyn Taylor

There are lots of tool brands that will work well for your build, including Milwaukee, Makita, Dewalt, Bosch. Pick a brand and stay with it so you won't have different battery chargers. All of these images are just for suggestions. Craigslist is a good place to look for ones that are not beat up and that are close to you. Don't drive 40 miles to save ten bucks.

PERFECT FOR TRIMMING 2X4'S	**NICE TO HAVE IF YOU NEED IT**	**8-PENNY AND 16-PENNY NAILER**
16 GAUGE STAPLER FOR USE WITH SIPS	**THIS IS THE SMALLER ONE BUT LOTS OF POWER TO DRIVE**	**9/16" X 4" LONG WITH 3/8" SHANK**
PRY BAR	**SCRAPER PRY BAR**	**9/16" IRWIN SPEEDBORE**

GREAT FOR TRIMMING

DON'T BUY A SMALL ONE LIKE THE BOTTOM ONE

THE TYPE WITH THE FRACTIONS WILL HELP

20 OZ SIZE FOR SIP MASTIC

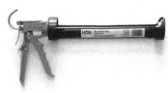

STANDARD SIZE • BUY A GOOD ONE • YOU'LL USE IT A LOT

SPEED SQUARE

FRAMING HAMMER

CHALK LINE REEL

HAMMER TACKER FOR WRB AND UNDERLAYMENT

2" X 27' FLAT HOOK END

MAKE SURE THAT ALL OF YOUR AIR HOSE FITTINGS MATCH

HYBRID HOSES ARE THE NEW BEST HOSE

CHAPTER THREE
Trailers

TRAILERS

"It is the unknown around the corner that turns my wheels."
- Heinz Stucke

WHY ARE YOU BUILDING ON A TRAILER?

- Is it so you can haul it around every weekend to a different camp site? *Probably not*.

- Is it to avoid having to pay large permitting fees and meet building codes? *Maybe*.

- Is it to allow you flexibility to move with new life and work opportunities? *Could be*.

LET'S START WITH SOME BASIC TERMINOLOGY.

Gross Vehicle Weight (GVW): The total weight that a trailer can haul, including the weight of the trailer itself. If your trailer has two 5,000 lb. axles, it has a GVW of 10,000 lbs., but only if the tires and hitch are also rated for that load at a minimum.

Load Rating: An assigned numerical value that indicates the relative load carrying capacity of various items, such as hitches, receivers, balls, tires. These critical items have been tested by a third party laboratory, where they effectively destroy it while measuring how much force it took to do so. They then divide the number by a safety factor. This gives you some confidence that when you hook a 7,000 lb. tiny house to a hitch of the same load rating or higher, it won't break and leave you stranded, if not worse.

Tongue: The front angled part of the trailer.

Hitch Jack: The jack with a crank handle used to raise the trailer off of the hitch ball.

Break-Away Kit: A device that will automatically apply the brakes to the trailer in the unlikely event that the trailer becomes unhooked from the towing vehicle.

Outriggers: Arm extensions or brackets that increase the width of the available building platform.

Cross Members: The steel angle, channel or tubing that connects the two sides of the main frame together at specific intervals.

Stabilizer Jacks: Small jacks on the four corners of a trailer to keep it level so it doesn't bounce around when you walk on it.

D-Rings: Places to secure tie downs when your THoW is permanently settled.

STYLES OF TRAILERS

Deck Over: This is where the deck of the trailer (i.e. the floor) is above the wheels and the tires. This is not used often because the height of the deck is usually between 30" and 36".

Deck Between: This is the most common for THoW's, where the fenders protrude into the deck area. There are three ways that trailer builders extend the width beyond the frame:

1. Some use steel angle on each side of the main frame.
2. Others build a framework of steel tube around the main frame.
3. Some use steel tube or Z metal outriggers protruding from the main frame.

Gooseneck or 5th Wheel: A trailer, usually for heavier loads, where the tongue of the trailer attaches to a coupler mounted above the axle on a truck bed.

SIZES OF TRAILERS

Although there is some variation among states as to the maximum size for a trailer with a load on it (i.e. THoW or RV), the general consensus in the THoW world is that the width should not exceed 8'-6"; the height 13'-5"; and the length 36 feet.

In most states an oversize permit is available and required for 9' wide trailers and runs between $10 and $50 and doesn't require any signs or flag cars.

NECESSARY CONSIDERATIONS

A THoW trailer needs to meet several criteria:

- It should be as light as possible to allow more weight on/in the structure and still remain within its GVW.

- It must be strong enough to support the loads imposed on it by your structure and the things you put into it (i.e. appliances, furniture, etc.). These loads should be calculated for a static state when your home is set up with the stabilizer jacks in use, as well as for the dynamic loads imposed on it during transport when you hit a bump, go around a corner or stop quickly.

- It should have a power braking system necessary to stop it safely when it is fully loaded.

- It must provide a solid foundation for the tiny house floor system.

- It should be designed to properly integrate a system for attaching the floor and the walls to it without rotting out. Any vintage trailer rebuilder will tell you about the rotted floor in old trailers.

DESIGN CRITERIA

Everyone wants the floor of their tiny home to be as low as possible for two mains reasons:

1. It simply makes it easier to get in and out of your home with less steps.

2. The lower the floor is, the more space you have at your disposal before running into the upper height limit.

There are a couple of ways to accomplish this:

> **Built-In:** The floor system is built in between the trailer main frame. This is very common.

> **Built-On:** The structure is built directly on top of the trailer frame and dropped axles are used to lower the floor.

In my opinion, the **Built-On** system is advantageous for several reasons, including:

- It allows for full insulation out to the edge (where Built-In usually stops between the main frame rails).

- The trailer cross members *become* the floor joists so no additional lumber is needed.

- It's easier to build and is the best application for using SIPs.

And it costs about the same when you factor out the additional framing. The floor might be about an inch higher, but all in all I still recommend it for the insulation gain.

See the drawing in the Bonus Material.

Every trailer manufacturer thinks their system for building is the best, otherwise they would be doing it another way. They are trailer manufacturers, however, and not homebuilders. They may not have a holistic or system's approach to the whole endeavor. And it's pretty much a given that they have not taken any green building or building science classes.

LOADS

Now let's think about the load on a tiny house trailer. Where does it come from?

The building load is comprised of the dead load of the roof, walls, windows and door, where one-half of the roof load transfers to each of the long walls.

When this modern wave of Tiny Houses on Wheels first started, they really were small. They were built on top of the trailer's main frame rails at about 7 feet wide. That worked out well to support the load.

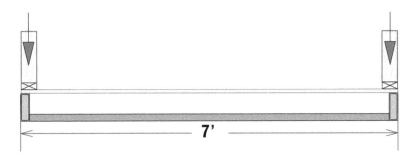

Then tiny houses started to grow in width (and length) from 7 feet to 8 feet, then 8 feet 4 inches, and now even up to 8 feet 9 inches. As the trailer gets wider there is an increased 'moment' where the force tries to spread the trailer frame apart.

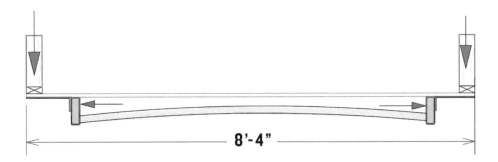

With these wider tiny houses with low cross members, the roof and walls are cantilevered off the main frame. This causes the axial force to bow the cross members. That is not a problem as long as you design a mechanism to counteract it: high cross members that resist the bending load.

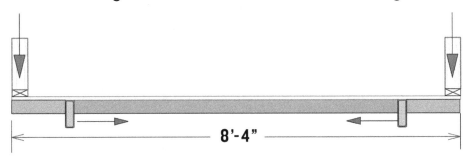

SIDE WALL LOAD EXAMPLE WITH POUNDS PER LINEAL FOOT (LBS/LINFT)

Let's take an 8'x24' THoW with a Single Slope Side-to-Side roof and do the numbers.

Assuming a Dead load of 10 lbs. for framing and roofing material and a 30-lb. Live load for snow:

Roof: 8 x 24 = 192 square feet x 40 lbs. = 7,680 lbs.
                7,680 divided by 2 = 3,840 lbs. to each wall
                3,840 divided by 24 feet = 160 lbs/LinFt

Walls: 24 ft x 10 ft (avg. height) = 240 square feet
                240 x 11 lbs/sq.ft. = 2,640 lbs per wall
                2,650 divided by 24 = 110 lbs/LinFt

Windows and Door: let's say another 10 lbs/LinFt

The total load onto the edge of the cantilevered trailer frame is
280 LBS PER LINEAR FOOT.

8' X 24' TRAILER	(A) SQ. FT.	(B) DEAD LOAD (lbs / sq. ft.)	(C) LIVE LOAD (lbs /sq. ft.)	(D) TOTAL LOAD PER SIDE (A x (B+C)/2)	POUNDS PER LINEAR FOOT (D/24)
ROOF	192	10	30	3,840	160
WALLS	240	11 (at 10' avg. height)		2,640	110
WINDOWS & DOOR					10
TOTAL LOAD PER LINEAR FOOT ON THE EDGE OF THE CANTILEVERED TRAILER FRAME:					280

We can design our trailer to meet the load above in a static mode, but know we still need to apply a dynamic load to be sure it's a strong enough frame when it hits a pothole traveling at 60 mph.

The ANSI Park Model code tells us to build the floor system for 30 lbs Live load. This is how much the floor system on top of the trailer frame needs to support in the middle of the floor.

Has your trailer manufacturer taken this information into account? Have they run the numbers?

HOUSE TRAILER

ROOF SL = 35 PSF
FLOOR LL = 30 PSF

ROOF DL   MTL   = 1.3
           SIP   = 3.5 ⎱ 7 PSF   IF ³/₈ PLYWD = 7.2
           SHEETROCK = 2.2

WALL DL   PLY/SIDE = 1.5
           SIP   = 3.5 ⎱ 7.2 PSF
           SHTRCK   = 2.2   USE 7.2 FOR ALL

FLR DL   ¾   = 2.3
           FOAM   = .5
           ½ PLY   = 1.5   ⎱ 7.3 PSF
           TUBE STEEL = 2.0
           FLR FINISH WGHT = 1.0

8'-4" WIDTH
ROOF LOAD = 4.17 × 7.2 = 30 PLF DL / 146 PLF SL
WALL DEAD LOAD = 8 (7.2) = 58 PLF

OUT RIGGER
                          DL   SL
          P = 2(30+58)/146 = 176/292 = 468 TL

          M = 468 × 6" = 2808 f_b = 2808/.87 = 3227 PSI

    F_b = 46000 × .6 = 27600 PSI >> 3227 PSI   OK EVEN IF WELDED
                                                    CONNECTION.

TORSION TAKEN IN BEARING BY 2½ CROSS
    t_v = 2808/.8 = 3510 PSI   OK

2½ ∅ CROSS MEMBER   SPAN = 80"   LOAD = 2(30/7.2) = 60/15
    M = 5000 "lb   M/s = 5000/.8 = 6250 << 27600 OK
    Δ = $\frac{.5 (6.25)(80)^4}{384 (29E6)(1.0)}$ = .115   L/695 OK

A CAUTION ABOUT USED TRAILERS

The internet is full of stories of people finding a utility trailer or a car hauler in the blackberry bushes behind a barn to use for building their tiny house. It's possible it may be usable *if* you can verify the GVW. Even then, if it's been out of service sitting in the weather for some time, it will need to be pulled apart to rebuild the brakes and check the bearings. It may also very well need to be rewired. These are not too hard if you know how to do the work yourself.

Other stories tell of dismantling an old RV in order to use the trailer. This is almost always a bad idea. RV trailers DO NOT have the high-capacity GVW to handle the load of a stick-built tiny house. If you are going to spend up to a year of your life and $20-40,000, you should seriously consider building on a trailer designed specifically for a Tiny House on Wheels.

LICENSING YOUR TRAILER

Unless you are a Park Model or RV manufacturer you will most likely be registering your trailer as just that - a flatbed trailer. Don't complicate your life; register your trailer before you start the build. Some states may require you to bring the trailer to their office to obtain a title and registration. If you haul it in there with a Tiny House already on it, you could be opening a can of worms.

In some states folks are able to have their THoW registered as a Park Model RV when it is finished. That is great if you can do it. You will want to check with your state to see if that is the route you want to go.

Resources:
Bonus Material
Department of Motor Vehicles

"May you have a strong foundation when the winds of change shift...and may you be forever young."

- Bob Dylan

CHAPTER FOUR
Floor | Walls | Roof

FLOOR | WALLS | ROOF

"If you don't build your dream,
someone will hire you to build theirs."
- Tony Gaskin

There are many things to think about when designing and building the envelope or "shell" of your new tiny home. Considering all that it needs to do, at the very least it must . . .

- Support the loads imposed on it from its own weight and the forces of nature acting upon and against it (e.g. wind, snow, ice, earthquake, etc.).

- Remain safe and secure traveling on the road at 60 MPH and potentially hitting a pothole along the way.

- Keep out the rain and the wind.

- Be energy-efficient and comfortable.

- Let in some light and fresh air.

There are several ways you can construct the shell of your new home. You could build it with studs, made of either wood or steel, or use Structural Insulated Panels.

Building with studs can provide the necessary load prerequisites, but it's not so good for insulation. It's always pretty labor intensive, so you need to ask yourself some good questions if you are considering going this route. Are you a framer or do you have a friend who is? Have you ever worked with steel studs? Do you know someone who does? I'm not going to go into how to frame here as there are hundreds of articles and books that go into great detail on the subject.

Structural insulated panels (SIPs), on the other hand, are prefabricated in large panels and can be assembled in one to two days with the proper tools and a little physical power. In addition, they are more energy-efficient up front and since the work of SIP fabrication is done in a clean and dry factory, there is less waste and the accuracy of the finished product is usually higher. SIPs also work very well for the floor and the roof.

This is why I recommend building with SIPs, which I'll explain in more detail later in this chapter.

FLOOR

One of the primary concerns when building a THoW is how to properly connect the floor to the trailer. The ANSI A119.5 Park Model code says to use ⅜" lag bolts every 48 inches around the perimeter. Unfortunately, I've seen instances where in one case the company used only four ⅜" threaded rods welded to the trailer and in another only a few lag bolts along the long walls. I have seen some tiny house trailers with NO provisions for attaching the floor. Remember, you can build better than code. I recommend - at a minimum - using 3/8" bolts with bearing plates and washers at 24" to 32" OC (on center). It doesn't add much weight, costs only pennies more, and provides a lot of peace of mind.

Another major concern using a trailer as the building platform is how to address the fact that water vapor in the air condenses when it comes into contact with steel. It is imperative that the wood in your floor system is separated from the steel of your trailer. To do so I urge the use of pressure-treated wood or a non-sweating material (e.g. rubber or foam) designed specifically for this purpose. If you don't, your floor will ROT. I have seen lots of THoWs with untreated wood going right against the steel of the trailer. Many manufacturers even build with steel pans in them. I understand that from a trailer manufacturer's standpoint this may seem like a good way to protect the underfloor of your home, but keep in mind that these manufacturers work with steel every day so of course they would reach for a steel solution. The problem is that this approach creates an even larger condensing pan that will introduce water into your floor system.

The best way I have found to break the 'condensing connection' is with ½" pressure-treated plywood; it allows you to still make a strong mechanical connection between the floor and the trailer. And as the Park Model code also requires protection from rodents, the pressure-treated plywood serves this purpose as well. I know it costs more, but this is the foundation; if it rots, you have a real problem! On a positive note from an environmental standpoint, the materials in PT plywood have also changed in the last few years. (See Pressure Treated Lumber for more information.)

WALLS

There are 'prescriptive' formulas for building with either wood or steel studs or SIPs listed in the International Residential Code (IRC). The Park Model code also has standards for using wood studs for a building that needs to withstand 70 MPH winds and a minimum 25-pound snow load. I have heard but just don't feel comfortable with 'by guess or by golly' or rules of thumb or, even worse, "that's the way gramps showed me how to do it." If you are going to spend your time and money to build your home, please make sure it is designed and built right.

I mentioned above that I'm not a big fan of building with studs. With 2'x4' stud framing, the actual wall is 3-½" thick; inserting fiberglass or rockwool results in an insulation value of about R-13. Use foam instead and that value could even get as high as R-16; that is, however, only where that insulation is not interrupted by a stud. At R-1 per inch for each 2'x4' wood stud, there is a significant reduction in the 'total wall' thermal value.

For example, a 10-foot high by 24-foot long THoW wall framed at 16" OC has 19 studs in it. At 1-1/2" each that's a total of 28-1/2 inches of solid wood, not even counting any window and door framing and headers.

I do believe building with SIPs makes more sense. A 4-½" SIP wall with white EPS (expanded polystyrene) foam provides an R-16 insulation value; the newer GPS (graphite polystyrene) grey foam provides an even higher R-20 value. Due to their inherent structural strength, building with SIPs also allows for fewer studs and headers, thereby maintaining a higher 'total wall' thermal value. In addition to the reduced thermal bridging with SIPs construction, they are also relatively airtight and as a result you end up with a less drafty and more comfortable home.

ROOF

Every building element that we use in the USA has been tested and re-tested to assign design load values. These values are published in the IRC and other books and tables. As an example, from the IRC 2015 version, a roof system built with 2'x6' SPF (spruce-pine-fir) lumber at a specific gravity of .50 spaced at 16" OC (on-center) can support 30 psf (pounds per square foot) with a span of up to 9'-4". At 12" OC you can span up to 10'-3" and support the same load. The ANSI code also has similar tables for headers and floor joists. And you can always build better than code.

What I'm asking for in this chapter is to make sure that *someone* is checking the numbers and, if applicable, checking the code to assure that your investment of time and money is not going to be lost.

I don't care if you have your home inspected and/or certified. I do care that it is built in a manner that makes it safe for the people living in it and for anyone following you down the highway.

BUILDING WITH SIPS

Stud construction dictates that someone needs to know how to translate architectural drawings into the placement of individual pieces of lumber according to accepted practices.

Building with SIPs is different. It starts by converting those same architectural drawings into shop drawings showing the dimensions and where windows and doors are placed. The shop drawings are used to fabricate the panels, which are then assembled onsite using the accepted construction practices for doing so.

When I'm designing with SIPs, I typically use 8-foot wide panels for the floor and walls. A 4-1/2" thick panel weighs about 3.3 pounds per square foot, so an 8-foot wide panel that is 8 feet tall (i.e. 64 square feet) weighs about 211 pounds. Four people who can each lift 50 pounds are easily able to maneuver it into place.

If you think about the average 24-foot tiny house, this means there will be three panels for the floor, eight panels for the walls and then six or seven 4-foot wide panels for the roof.

The initial cost of structural insulated panels will usually be a little more than building with studs. Part of that cost is paying people in the factory to manufacture and then cut the panels to size with the openings for windows and a door. You can save some money on your project by buying all the additional lumber that's needed for plates and bucks and installing it yourself.

The upside of building with SIPs includes the improved air-tightness and energy efficiency as well as the speed with which the envelope can go together. Usually a THoW with SIPs can be assembled in a two-day house raising.

WINDOWS & DOORS

"A house without books is like a room without windows."

- Horace Mann

WINDOWS

There are several parts to a window and it's necessary to know the terminology to make sure you order correctly. They are the glass, the frame, the style and the sash.

No matter where you live, your windows should always be double-paned (i.e. have two panes of glass). It's 2018, after all, and we should not be going backwards on energy efficiency. We can debate lots of things from there, like how far apart the panes should be and what kind of gas, if any, to put in between them, and what coatings to put on the glass and which side it should go on. I'll let you do your own research on those details because it can take days.

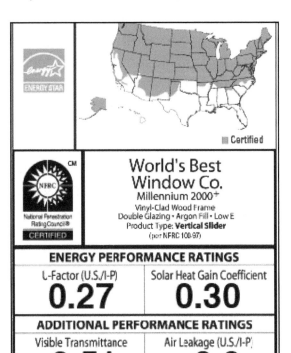

ENERGY PERFORMANCE RATINGS	
U-Factor (U.S./I-P)	Solar Heat Gain Coefficient
0.27	0.30

ADDITIONAL PERFORMANCE RATINGS	
Visible Transmittance	Air Leakage (U.S./I-P)
0.51	≤0.3

Windows are rated for their thermal performance in what's known as U-value, which tells us how fast energy moves through an element. This is the inverse of R-value, which tells how the element resists the flow of energy. The more energy efficiency you want, the lower the U-value and the higher the R-value.

The bottom line is that windows are very good at letting light in and very poor at being insulators.

For instance, if we converted window performance to an R-value, a single pane would be R-1, a double pane would be R-2, and even a triple pane would only be about R-3. With the addition of gasses and coatings, you can get a little better performance. There are windows available today with R-5 and even higher, but no one I know can afford them. So let's switch back to U-value, because that is what you will see on window labels.

Washington and Oregon are leaders in energy efficient standards for homes and they have both moved over the years from U-32 down to U-30.

WINDOW FRAMES

Window frames are constructed of vinyl, fiberglass, wood or wood-clad. Vinyl is the most prevalent due to its low cost, but it's not my favorite choice since it has some environmental drawbacks, including the emission of toxic fumes during production, so it's not a healthy factory to work in. A more recent window frame material is fiberglass, which is actually lighter and may be even more durable than vinyl.

A great option, if you can afford them, are wood-clad windows, which are incredibly attractive. These have wood trim on the interior and a lower maintenance option on the exterior, which is often aluminum. I have found some great deals on both fiberglass and wood-clad windows on sites like Craigslist.

The biggest consideration when designing for windows and their placement in a tiny home is actually the amount of glass, also known as glazing. I know you see tiny houses on TV shows and in blogs with a whole wall of glass, but too much glass will make the building either overheat or be difficult to heat depending on the climate.

A good rule of thumb is to have about 15-20% of the floor area in glazing. For example, an 8x24 tiny house is 192 square feet, which would equate to a total of between 28 and 38 square feet of glass divided into as many windows as desired.

Window size is also an important consideration when building on a smaller scale. I wish I could turn off the part of my brain that thinks about engineering and style and scale, but I can't.

When a window becomes too wide for the wall framing above it to safely carry the roof load, it's time to put in a framing element called a 'header.' There are two challenges with this element. The first is that it is usually a large solid hunk of wood, which is now another thermal bridge. The second is that a 'point load' is created on each end of the header where the roof load is concentrated. On a ground-bound home (i.e. one with a foundation) this doesn't present a problem; simply add a big chunk of concrete with some rebar to the foundation and the load is transferred to the ground. On a THoW trailer we don't have that luxury. Trailers are designed to have a uniform load equally distributed along the edges.

Yes, I know you saw that really cool house on TV or on the internet, but did they take this information into consideration? Who knows, but I don't make up this engineering stuff. It just is. I'd love to see one of those THoWs several years after it's been completed and after a couple of harsh winters with heavy snow on it.

WINDOW STYLES

The STYLE of a window has to do with how it looks and operates. The most common styles include:

> Fixed: The window doesn't open (used in all types of homes).

> Slider: The sash moves from side to side (usually contemporary homes).

> Single Hung: The bottom sash moves up and down (more traditional designs).

> Double Hung: Both sashes move; the upper moves down and the lower moves up.

> Casement: The sash cranks out on a vertical hinge, either left or right (modern homes).

> Awning: The sash cranks out on a horizontal upper hinge (also modern homes).

Lastly, the **SASH** of a window is the part with the glass in it.

You can mix or match styles, but I think it usually works best if you decide on one based on the home's design, such as Fixed and Single/Double Hung for a traditional cabin look.

DOORS

The newest and now better insulated doors are made of fiberglass and steel with foam insulation. They typically have a U-value of around .20, which translates to an R-5. You will still find lots of wood doors, but keep in mind that they only have an insulation value of around R-1.

The door is the entry to your tiny house, which will become your home. I like a door that says WELCOME. It is also one of the first indicators of who lives there. Think about what you want to express. This is one of those areas where I encourage clients to take their time and spend a couple more dollars if need be to get the 'right' door, even if that means putting in a temporary door until their budget allows.

Speaking of right - doors can open in either direction (left or right) and swing to the inside or the outside. I often design tiny houses with the door swinging to the outside to save precious floor space. (A side benefit is the security factor since they can't be kicked in.) If you choose to have your door swing into the space, be sure it will swing out of the way of the main traffic pattern.

Please DO NOT buy windows or a door until you have a design! Okay, maybe you can buy that really cool one and then drive the design around it. Just acknowledge that you have put yourself into a design box very early on in the process. That's okay if you truly know what you want.

If you buy a window or a door before you have a design, you will feel obliged to use it, and you'll start poking holes in your building just because it's that particular shape and size. If you don't mind that your home ends up looking a bit hodge podge, then maybe it doesn't matter. Eclectic can be a style just like steampunk or a total-recycled look, something you'll be proud to have accomplished.

The key here is to think about it - before you start - so when it's finished you can stand back and say "Wow, that is just what I had in mind!"

Lastly, here are a few important points to keep in mind when shopping for windows and doors:

- Make sure you buy windows that are designed for new construction. That means they have fins, which are the 1-1/2" protrusions from each edge that are used for installing them. You can use the retrofit style, but you'd better know what you are doing to keep out the water.

- Get acquainted with the terminology and dimensions for ordering windows:

  - The 'call out' size is what contractors and window manufacturers use. Width comes before height: for example, 3/0 x 4/0 is a window that is 3'-0" wide x 4'-0" tall.

  - The 'rough opening' is the size of the framed hole in the wall for the window to fit into; it is usually ½ inch larger in both directions than the window unit itself.

  - With vinyl and fiberglass, the actual window will be ½" smaller than the call out size.

  - With aluminum wood-clad windows (and doors), the width of the jamb comes into play because the interior jamb is an integral part of the unit.

With respect to doors, keep in mind that the jamb depth will vary depending upon what material is used to finish the wall.

I would strongly recommend buying a pre-hung door. If you find a door you really like without an installed jamb, you can take it to a door shop and have it hung for around $100-150 and it's well worth every penny. Trust me on this one; properly hanging a door onsite is very challenging, even with experience.

Resources: Energy.gov

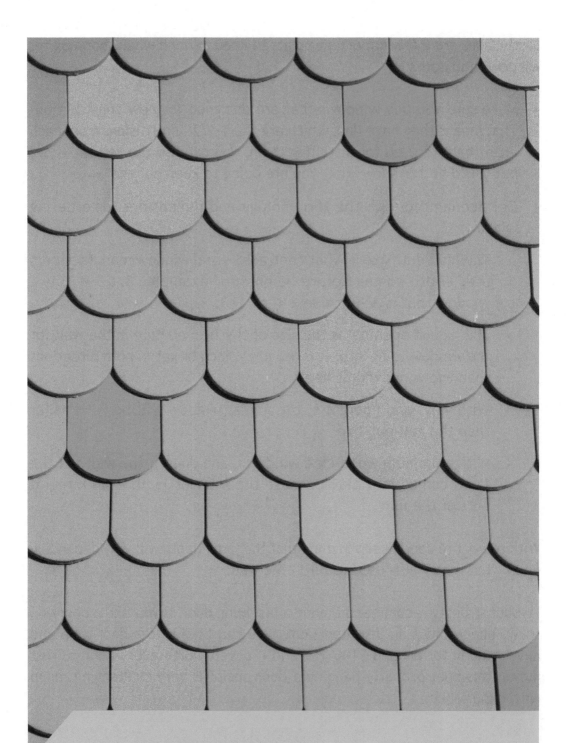

CHAPTER SIX
Roofing

ROOFING

"The sky's the limit if you have a roof over your head."
- Sol Hurok

What makes the best roofing?....*It depends.*

The choice of roofing material depends on your roof design, your climate, your snow load, your expertise and your budget. It can be one of the most difficult decisions to make on your project due to its visibility.

That said, here are the most common options that work best for THoWs:

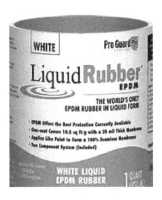

Roll-on Liquid Membrane: This is often used on commercial buildings. It is the least costly and the easiest to apply (with a brush and roller) and weighs about 1/4 psf (pound per square foot). I know it's not very pretty, but so what if your driver is least cost or your home is in the middle of 40 acres where no one is going to see it. You can even install another style over it later.

Roll-on Membrane (EPDM rubber or TPO glued down): This is also a very reasonably priced solution and weighs about ½ to 1 psf. It is also a very durable product that can stand up to the harsh UV rays of the sun. Commonly available in black or white, TPO also comes in grey and tan. You will need to find a commercial roofing installer that will sell you some of their smaller pieces or find a commercial roofing distributor who would be willing to sell to you.

Shingles: These can be cost effective, but they are very heavy at about 3 psf. If you used up your weight budget with granite counter tops this might put you over the limit of your GVW.

 Metal: This roof is one of the most durable; it can last over 50 years. It also takes the most skill to install. Metal roofing is sold by the gauge and is not what you'd think: for example, 29 ga. is thinner than 26 ga. There are lots of colors and profiles to choose from. Be advised that the less expensive barn metal has nice wide sheets but the exposed fasteners will eventually leak; be sure to read the directions - the screws go into the flat and not through the ribs on a barn metal roof.

If choosing metal roofing, I recommend spending a few dollars more and using the 'SnapLock' hidden fastener style. Although 24 gauge is available, 26 gauge is plenty thick enough since you'll have full sheeting under the metal. The steel comes with several kinds of finishes; in my experience KYNAR is a good one that doesn't fade. Another advantage to SnapLock roofing is that it is very easy to mount solar panels to with S-5 clips and only weighs about one pound per square foot.

Skylights are a fun addition to a roof but, depending on your choice of roofing, can be a challenge to flash correctly to avoid leaks.

Whichever material you choose make sure to read and follow the manufacturer's installation instructions. There is no one who wants this part of your project to succeed more than the roofing manufacturer.

Don't stress; breathe and go.
There are no wrong decisions,
only opportunities to learn.

CHAPTER SEVEN
Siding

SIDING

"The sun never knew how great it was
until it hit the side of a building."
- Louis Kahn

What makes the best siding?....*It depends.*
You're probably starting to see a pattern here.

With stud construction you need a sheathing product (e.g. OSB or plywood) to give rigidity to the walls of your home. With SIPs, the outside sheathing is already an integral part of the panel. In either case it is essential that the sheathing resist the environmental forces that will be exerted upon it. It must be protected from the elements, which is why we install cladding - or siding - on all buildings.

We have also learned through experience that it is very important to install a weather resistive barrier ('WRB') between the structural sheathing and the siding. You may know this type of product as 'housewrap', but today it could even be applied as a liquid (see *StowGuard* for an example). Since any type of siding will be penetrated by water at some point in its lifetime, the WRB acts as a backup for maintaining the integrity of your exterior wall sheathing.

As mentioned in the Building Science section of Chapter Two, a more recent recommendation to extend the life of a building is the use of a rain screen system. The small space created by the rain screen permits air to flow between the siding and the sheathing allowing any water that does get in to dry out. A beneficial side effect of this system is that any paint you apply to your siding will also last a lot longer.

Unfortunately, this is an area where I have seen folks try to save a few dollars or cut corners to speed up the close-in. Since durability is one of my drivers, I encourage everyone to seriously consider spending roughly $400-600 more to double the expected life of their investment. As an instructor at a JLC-Live class once said, "The more it rains in your area, the more you need a rain screen system."

So now let's talk about the actual siding. It's good to know that you don't have to do all or nothing. You may have already noticed that some of the nicest looking THoWs have a thoughtful or even eclectic mix of siding options.

The least cost and easiest to install siding is a plywood product like T1-11. It comes in various grades and thicknesses as well as several patterns. Explore the internet and you find anything and everything you'll need to know.

Although they're a bit more expensive, cedar and redwood are favorites here on the West Coast for their lighter weight. These wood products come in lots of different styles as you'll see pictured here. Look around to see what is available in your local area.

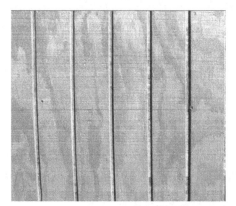

EXAMPLES OF TI-II PLYWOOD

CEDAR   **REDWOOD**

Another choice made by some tiny home owner-builders is corrugated metal siding. Either alone or mixed with other mediums and artfully placed, it can be quite attractive. In spite of what you might have seen on television, cement siding is NOT a good choice for a THoW. It is just too heavy to even be considered.

The outside is all buttoned up to the weather. You deserve a break.
This is a good time to take a weekend off.

PLUMBING

"Acting is not an important job in the
scheme of things. Plumbing is."
- Spencer Tracy

LET'S KEEP IT SIMPLE: WATER IN, WATER OUT.

It's important to start with some of the basic terminology:

- Potable *(poe-tuh-bull)* water is drinkable water.
- Gray water is water from sinks and showers.
- Black water is water from toilets.

What is your potable water source? In most situations it is going to be a well or a municipal water system, connected to your THoW with a hose joined to a spigot. There are a couple of other ways to get water into your tiny home. The first is simply by bucket. It's amazing how little water you'll find you actually need when you carry it in - at 8.36 pounds per gallon, a 5-gallon bucket weighs over 40 pounds!

Another source of potable water is via a rain water catchment system. There is a lot more involved in this type of system than you might initially think. First, you can only capture water from roofing that will not add pollutants to the water (e.g. steel). Second, you will need to flush off the first few gallons when it starts to rain just to keep dirt out of your storage. Third, you'll need to store the water safely to keep it potable. And fourth, you'll need a system to kill any bacteria before you drink it. Oh, and you'll also need to pump it from the storage tank to the point of use with enough pressure to be able to use it effectively.

As noted above, water is heavy. If you are not traveling with your tiny house where you need to keep it on board, you could store it outside, even elsewhere on your property. You could also have a hybrid system, where only a small amount is stored on board.

The key to remember with almost any mechanical system is that you can break it down to its various components. This has all been done before and today the parts and pieces are readily available. I like to start with the simple and then move toward the more complex, noting that most of these types of systems can also be added on later.

Resources:
Camel Water Cycle System

WATER IN

POTABLE WATER - HOOK UP

This is where we start borrowing from our RV cousins. There are many types of hoses on the market, but as far as your THoW water hose is concerned, you need to select one that is designed specifically for drinking water. Garden hoses (typically green, but now available in a variety of colors) are unsuitable because not only can they harbor bacteria, but they also add chemicals to the water as it passes through, especially on warm/hot days. Hoses that are safe to use for a potable water supply are usually transparent or white and clearly state on a label or the hose itself that it is safe for drinking water use.

Even a simple setup for connecting to a municipal water source has several components, so let's look at it going backwards. First, connect a short hose to the fresh water inlet on the exterior of your THoW. Next, add a course water filter to keep sand and dirt out of your plumbing. Now add a pressure regulator to assure proper flow, and finally, add whatever length of hose is necessary to get to the city water inlet. After actually hooking up this type of system, I recommend taking it back apart and then, starting at the municipal source, turning on the water and letting it run through each piece before connecting the next one just to give it a little time to clean out.

Now that you have the water up to and through the wall, it needs to be distributed to the sinks and shower. The most common supply piping is called PEX; it is lightweight and very easy to work with. I like to use two colors for my runs: blue for the cold water and red for the hot. I'm not going to expand on plumbing with PEX here as there are already many books and videos on that subject readily available.

Resources:
Supply House
RV Parts Country

HOT WATER

Simple is good when it comes to heating water. There are always electric water heaters. With this type you need to find a suitable location for it in your THoW and then plumb those hot water lines around the building to the fixtures in the sinks and shower.

A better option might be an on-demand 'tankless' model that only heats up the water as it flows through it when needed. Some models even have a small tank holding up to a few gallons of hot water ready for use. By installing small 120V on-demand models in the bathroom and under the kitchen sink, you only need to run cold water to each location and connect to the heater with a short pipe to the sink or shower. Check your local water temperature where it comes out of the ground. An electric on-demand unit can only raise the water so many degrees at the flow rate that you will want: shower >2 GPM (gallons per minute); bath sink: .5 GPM; and kitchen sink: 1.5 GPM.

If you are going to have a propane gas piping system (see Heating in Chapter Twelve), you might as well have a gas water heater. I would recommend an on-demand unit similar to one of these:

There are only a few that are sized appropriately for a tiny house. Since they need to be vented to the outside, many people install them outside in a covered 'dog house' on the tongue of the trailer. This can lead to another challenge, however, since the water in them can freeze and ruin the heater. If you are in a frigid climate, be sure to install it inside. If you are in a mild climate, install it inside or out.

WATER HEATER SETTINGS

The key with any water heater is making sure the temperature rise and water flow rate it provides can meet your needs, and this can get confusing. What are the heater's BTU output and maximum GPM (gallons per minute) flow rate at your water inlet temperature? For example, if you have water at the inlet at 50°F and for a shower you are going to want 120°F water, you'll need a 70° rise in temperature. You'll also want a flow rare of about 2 GPM.

If it's an on-demand water heater, you'll also want to know the minimum GPM activation flow rate and the minimum flow rate to be activated.

There also at least a few other things to consider, including physical size, installation/clearance and venting requirements, and freeze protection.

Plumbing and electrical are a little like asking for directions for some guys. Trust me; it's okay to ask a professional for help figuring out this stuff.

WATER OUT

GREY WATER

This is another one of those areas where we can borrow from the RV industry by using connectors and pipes that are designed for grey water removal. It is fairly simple using ABS piping. You'll want to combine all of the waste water runs from the sinks and shower into one pipe that can be easily disconnected for traveling.

It's important to think about where that grey water goes. Because of the soaps used in washing and bathing, grey water should not be used for watering food gardens. It can, however, be used for watering shrubs and ornamentals. It can also be run to a bioswale where the water will percolate into the soil.

BLACK WATER

Unless you are traveling all of the time, you will probably not have a black water tank onboard your THoW. One way to deal with black water is to have a hose or pipe that hooks directly into a septic tank or municipal system with the use of a sewage pumping system. Be aware that hooking to a municipal system can be very expensive and fraught with bureaucratic hurdles.

COMPOSTING TOILETS

Another way to deal with human waste is with a composting toilet. Doing so will greatly simplify your waste plumbing, however, you do need to answer a couple of key questions. Where will you empty the liquid waste? Where will you dispose of the solid waste?

With respect to solid waste, many composting toilets have a small fan that runs 24-7. Poop today, dry tomorrow. If you are on your own land it is pretty easy to set up a small composting bin just for the 'humanure.' Compost from this bin should only be used on ornamentals and shrubs. People put all kinds of drugs and other stuff in their bodies and it may not be healthy or suitable for growing food.

Liquid waste can be diluted and used on plants or if there is a toilet or mop sink available that hooks to a municipal sewage system you can empty it there. *(Don't ask, don't tell.)*

In the U.S. we throw millions of tons of human waste into the solid waste stream every day in the form of disposable diapers. That said, the powers that be can't seem to get their heads wrapped around someone dealing with their own waste. I say this to caution that you might not want to tell the county sanitation folks what you are doing. *Oops, there goes the old hippie again.* Better yet, check out the comprehensive site below on the legality in your state.

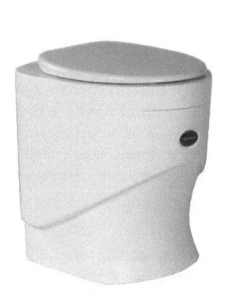 

Resources:
The Humanure Handbook: A Guide
to Composting Human Manure
Separett Composting Toilet
Shop Tiny Houses

"The ground's generosity takes in
our compost and grows beauty!
Try to be more like the ground."

- Rumi

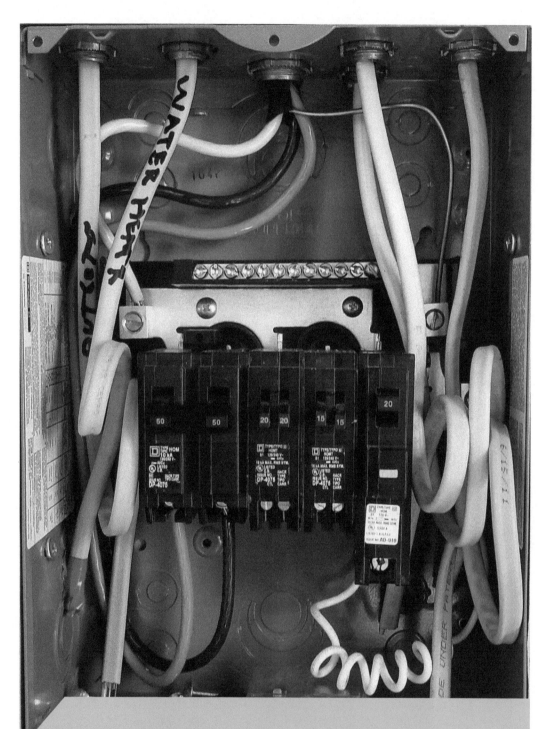

ELECTRICAL

"We believe that electricity exists because the electric
company keeps sending us bills for it, but we cannot
figure out how it travels inside wires."

- Dave Barry

As with the other chapters, I'll be discussing this subject from a high level
and then point you towards resources for digging down into the details.

Dealing with the electrical system is scary for a lot of folks and that is
probably a good thing. Even if you hire an electrician, you are going to need
to make some basic decisions to guide him or her. How much electricity
do you really need? Could you live with 6 outlets? How many light switches
do you want: 3 or 4? What about a separate circuit for your microwave,
toaster oven and/or induction cooktop?

Some of these are dictated by code; some are just a preference. The Park
Model code says we are to use the Fire Protection Agency Electrical code.
In the western U.S. we use the National Electric Code for homes built on
the ground. Fortunately, there isn't a lot of difference between them.

If you don't know what you are doing here, please get some professional help.
I wired my ground-bound home when we built it years ago. Knowing that
codes change over time, I asked a couple of friends for a recommendation
and paid a licensed electrician to come over and make sure I was doing it
right.

If you cut all the holes for outlets and switches, the rough-in part
shouldn't take more than a day or so. One thing I find helpful is to
have Loads like your bath exhaust fan, electric heater, and electric
water heater (if you are using one) installed before you begin. If they
are, it makes it easier to see where you are going with your wires.
If you are getting it inspected, leave the cover off the Load Center and
don't install switches and outlets until after the inspection.

TERMINOLOGY

Load Center: a steel box with breakers in it to distribute the electricity.

Breaker: an over-current switching device to control the flow of electricity.

Branch Circuit: a wire run from a breaker that provides power to the loads.

Outlet: the socket that you plug loads into.

Loads: the devices (e.g. outlets, lights, and appliances) that pull the electricity through the wires.

BACK TO THE BASICS

Let's start with a simple, standard 120V plug-in system. The first decision you have to make is to determine how much power will you need.

THE FOUR BASIC TERMS IN ELECTRICITY

Voltage (V): measured in volts
Current (I): measured in amps
Resistance (r): measured in ohms
Watts (W): units of power draw

Watts describe the rate at which electricity
is being used at any specific moment.

(Example: a 15-watt LED light bulb draws 15 watts
of electricity when it's turned on.)

A neat analogy to help understand these terms is to think of plumbing pipes. The voltage (V) is equivalent to the water pressure, the current (I) is equivalent to the flow rate, and the resistance (r) is the pipe size.

Oops, probably TMI already; keep reading -- it gets easier.

HOW MUCH IS ENOUGH?

Determining the voltage is easy because in the U.S. we use power at 120V Alternating Current (AC) at 60 cycles per second. So that decision is already made for us.

What you'll need to determine is how much electricity will be used at any given moment so the proper wires are installed correctly and the system will work properly. Because we have an electrical code in the U.S. that is widely recognized, and enforced, a lot of these decisions have been made for us on the basis of safety.

The code tells us - for good reason - that you can only run so many outlets off one circuit. For example, if you have 6 outlets and they all have something plugged into them and are turned on at the same time, the wire could get hot enough to start a fire. Obviously, nobody wants that.

So think about your power needs. If you are using electric appliances, you will need to know the watt usage or AMP draw for each of them in order to determine what size Load Center you will need. Take a look at your current electric bill. It's a good starting point for determining what size electric system you'll want to put in your tiny home.

PLUG AND PLAY

Actually getting the electricity into your tiny home is another place we can borrow from our RV cousins. The only decision to make here is whether you need a 30-amp or a 50-amp system. Whatever you decide will affect the equipment you purchase. My experience is that for a 16-20 foot tiny home, a 30-amp system is probably enough. For anything larger, I would use a 50-amp panel. The difference in cost is usually only a couple hundred dollars and you'll never regret having enough power available.

To make the connection to your source of electricity, you will need to start at the exterior wall of your tiny house with the correct electrical inlet receptacle (pedestal). The 30-amp and 50-amp receptacles are different so make sure to purchase the correct one.

LOAD CENTER   **30/50 AMP RV WIRE**   **PEDESTAL**

The cord that plugs into the power receptacle will be a twist lock connector that keeps out the weather and makes it difficult for the plug to come loose accidentally. You will obviously need a cord to connect from the source of the electricity to the tiny home.

Once connected to a power source, a heavy gauge wire will take the electricity from the inlet receptacle to your Load Center, where it can be further distributed to the various loads.

Resources:
Home Power Magazine
Tiny House Systems
Shop Tiny Houses

SOLAR ELECTRIC

*"I'd put my money on the sun and solar energy.
What a source of power! I hope we don't have to wait
until oil and coal run out before we tackle that."*
- Thomas Edison

Are you going to add a solar electric system either now or later? This is a big one as the cost of a photovoltaic (PV) system can run anywhere from about $3,000 to $6,000 or more. Although it is a separate system, there are some decisions you can make now that could make even a later installation much easier.

There are two main ways to use solar for your tiny home. One is 'grid-tied' where you rely on the electric grid to back you up when the sun doesn't shine. The other is 'off-grid' where you store your excess sun-gathered energy until you need it. With grid-tied you might think about ground mounting the PV panels or putting them on an accessory building in order to have enough surface area to mount them.

For off-grid, there are several pieces to the puzzle. In addition to the panels themselves, you also need the following parts:

- Batteries to store the electricity.
- A charge controller to stop charging the batteries when they are full.
- An invertor so you can plug 120V items into the power.
- A charger so you can fill the batteries from land power when you need to.

And don't forget all the properly sized wires to hook it all together.

There are plenty of books and resources for how to do this online. Or you can make it easy and call my friends at Backwoods Solar for answers to these questions. They have been helping folks get off-grid for decades and they have put together some basic systems in three sizes just for those of us in the THoW world.

Resources: <u>Backwoods Solar</u>   <u>Shop Tiny Houses</u>

CHAPTER TEN
Lofts & Stairs

LOFTS & STAIRS

"The vision must be followed by the venture. It is not enough to stare up the steps – we must step up the stairs."

- Vance Havner

Remember from the section on Codes in Chapter 2 that I've chosen to use the Park Model as a guideline for my design work: ANSI A119.5 Section 5 Construction Requirements.

This code requires headroom of 6'-6" with the exception that 50% of a defined space (e.g. a bathroom or under a loft) can be at 6'-0". Remember all codes are the minimum. I prefer a floor-to-loft joist height of 6'-8". It's essential to design a loft where the floor joists safely accommodate the load imposed by people sleeping or *not* sleeping as the case may be. It's also amazing to consider just how much 'stuff' seems to find its way up there, not the least of which are heavy books.

CALCULATIONS

For those of you reading this book who are self-proclaimed geeks, I have some fun tools to share with you. The American Wood Council has this handy, dandy tool called *Spancalc* for calculating the maximum horizontal span for most species of lumber. Here's how I use it to design a safe loft using the Park Model code parameters:

- Choose the species of wood to be used.
- Set the Size to 2x4.
- Change the Grade from Select Structural to No. 2 (unless you can find No. 1 locally).
- Leave the Member Type as Floor Joists.
- Set the Deflection Limit to L/360.
- Set the Spacing to 12.
- Set the Live Load (psf) to 30.
- Set the Dead Load (psf) to 10.
- Hit the Calculate button and scroll down to find the result.

When you've successfully worked it out, print a screen shot for your binder. It will be handy to include with any certification paperwork.

There are also applications available from the American Wood Council for your phone.

ACCESSING THE LOFT

Section 5-10.4 of the Park Model code covers stairways. In simple terms it says the steepest a set of steps can be is 12 inches up ('rise') with a 7-inch minimum depth ('run'). Those are very steep stairs with not much room for your feet. It says they must also be 20 inches wide. (I would prefer 16 inches for better utilization of a 4x8 sheet of plywood, but I can work with this number.) Just for comparison's sake, a ground-bound house, which is subject to the International Residential Code (IRC), limits the steepest stairway you can build to a 7-1/4" maximum rise and a 10-inch minimum run, almost the reverse.

Of course you can build as comfortable and/or elaborate a tiny house stairway as you wish, but it may take up more floor space. You'll find some clever examples in this section.

The usual method for determining the rise and run on any staircase requires a bit of trial and error to reach what's allowed by code. Start with the height from the finished floor below to the finished floor above (let's call it "X"). Next determine the length of floor space designated for that stairway ('Y'). Now choose a number for your desired 'rise' ("Z").

<u>EXAMPLE:</u>   X = 80"   Y = 60"   Z =12"
Divide X by Z to get the number of steps: 80 / 12 = 6.67 or 7 steps
Divide Y by 7 to get the run: 60 / 7 = 8.57" rounded to 8.5" for ease
The stairway is this case would be 7 steps with a 12" rise and an 8.5" run.

Alternatively, the Park Model code allows for a ladder to access the loft, which can be a good choice when space is limited. As stated in Park Model Code 5-10.5.1, a ladder shall have a 12-inch minimum rung width with a 10-inch to 14-inch spacing between rungs. The ladder shall support 300 pounds and be installed at an angle between 70 and 80 degrees. Since there is no depth called out for a tread, you can even use a regular round-rung ladder, but it really isn't much fun on bare feet.

The code also allows an alternating tread device: 5-10.4.2.3. Alternating tread devices shall be permitted as long as the width complies with code 5-4.1.1 (i.e. 20 inches). In this case, the tread minimum is 8-1/2 inches and the maximum rise is 8 inches.

When thinking about access to your loft, don't forget sites like Craigslist. I have seen some very cool ladders there; just make sure it fits within the above parameters.

Resources and tools:
American Wood Council
Block Layer
Bonus Material

HANDRAIL

This is for stairs, not ladders, but I think even ladders with stair treads ('sladders') can benefit from a handrail. According to ANSI A119.5, it shall be between 30" and 38" measured vertically from the nosing of the stair. Grip sizes shall have a cross-section diameter of 1-1/4 to 2 inches.

GUARDRAILS

Open sides of stairs shall have intermediate rails or balusters which do not permit the passage of an object 4" in diameter.

Lofts over 30" above the floor shall have a guardrail not less than 36" or one-half the height from the loft floor to the ceiling, whichever is less, with the same 4" object rule. There is a lot more interesting language in the Park Model code, but this will get you headed in the right direction. Much of this language is very similar to the IRC code.

MEANS OF ESCAPE

Also known as egress, this seems to be a big item of concern to the powers that be. The Park Model code addresses it this way: each loft shall have a minimum of one exit in addition to the staircase or ladder. This exit shall provide direct access to the exterior and comply with 3-2.2 and 3-2.6. The size of an alternate exit shall provide an opening of sufficient size to permit unobstructed passage of an ellipse generated by rotating about its minor axis an ellipse having a major axis of 24" and a minor axis of 17". Did you get all that? It does not mean that an 18" x 24" window will work. Once you subtract the frame and sash you will probably need at least a 30" x 24" window. A skylight that meets these size requirements could also work.

Put a smoke alarm with a ten-year battery up in the loft. It's easy to do and it's code.

What I've referred to above are just small excerpts from the Park Model RV code. Please obtain your own copy for the complete language.

Resources:
ANSI A119.5 (from the RVIA online store)
Escape Skylights

"Reuse is the original green collar job."

- MaryEllen Etienne

WALLS | TRIM | CEILING

"Aim for the sky and you'll reach the ceiling.
Aim for the ceiling and you'll stay on the floor."
- Bill Shankly

The interior finish of your walls and ceiling can make a dramatic statement about the style of your home.

If 'keep it simple' is your style, then 1/4" paneling over your framing could be a good fit. Make sure it is low-VOC (volatile organic compounds) for healthy indoor air quality. If you're building with SIPs, then the simple way is just to paint over the OSB. When I do that, I put on two coats of primer, sand lightly and then apply a coat or two of the finish paint - all low or no-VOC, of course. I find that a pad applicator works well for getting into the grain of OSB. I like the texture; I've had people compare it to strawbale.

There are lots of other materials that can add style to your home, like Salvage Works' WOW wall (see Resources). This can even be a recycled wood that you clean up yourself. Think old fencing, siding or flooring.

I have seen folks use sheetrock, but it is heavy and messy to finish. Metals can be a fun interior finish and you can mix it up with different finishes on separate walls. You might find enough material of one kind to do even one wall and then buy matching or contrasting new materials for another.

TRIM

Trim can really eat up time when you are finishing your home. By trim I mean everything from the material you use around your windows on the interior to make them look attractive to that little piece of quarter-round or something like it that closes the gap between a cabinet and the wall. Almost anywhere one material meets another will need a piece of trim or a bead of caulk to make it look the best.

WINDOW TRIM

This can be anything from drywall to a scrap of countertop to a piece of wood depending on the style you want for your home. Most of the time it is made from a length of 3/4" wood of some variety. With windows, especially, keep an open mind on materials. If you're on a tight budget a less expensive wood like pine or something cool you find on Craigslist works great. Most of the time you will want it to be 1/2" to 3/4" thick. You can even use a different material on the bottom sill (e.g. marble) and perhaps make it wider than the sides to give you a nice mini-shelf.

This is good place to do a "take off" of the dimensions you are going to need for the window trim, so if you find X number of linear footage of material you will know if it is going to be enough for all the windows. Or you can mix and match by using a different material for the upstairs windows.

FLOOR TRIM

Where the floor meets the wall is yet another location where you will usually need to add trim. The lumber yard is always happy to sell you wood for up to $20 per 8' or 10' length. If you have a table saw, however, it easy to cut down wider lengths of board and put a bevel on the edge.

Resources:
Salvage Works

"I have a motto on my bedroom wall:

'Obstacles are what you see when you

take your eye off the goal.'

Giving up is not my style. I just want

to do something that's worthwhile."

- Chris Burke

CHAPTER TWELVE
Appliances

APPLIANCES

"The most important thing in art is The Frame. For painting, literally; for other arts: figuratively - because without this humble appliance, you can't know where The Art stops and The Real World begins."
- Frank Zappa

There are some big decisions to be made here. Will you include a gas system in your home? If yes, then it opens up more options for appliances, but it also introduces more complexity. It means designing and installing another system from the gas storage bottles to the final connection to each appliance. How will you refill the gas tanks? How much will you use each week? It is not a bad thing, just some more things to think about. If you go all electric, it will be Plug and Play.

Does everything have to be new? I know it can be nice, but does it really matter if the goal is financial freedom. At this point in the build it is easy to get caught up in 'buy, buy, buy.' It's a good time to remember that Craigslist is full of used appliances at about half the cost of new and many are barely used. Start looking early so you can get the color and style you want. Make a list and start checking items off. Most appliances today slide in, so you can still get the new one, just later on.

REFRIGERATOR
Size does matter. Do you need a small one or a large unit? Measured in cubic feet, fridges come in an unbelievable variety. Keep it simple. For a lot of folks a small undercounter fridge with or without an ice-cube section is all they need. My vote is for a little larger fridge with a separate freezer compartment. At least try this size and if you decide you need a larger one, move up to the next size, but know that it won't fit under your counter.

MICROWAVE
I don't know about you, but mostly I use a microwave for (re)heating hot drinks or frozen entrees. Think about your needs and only get one if you really plan on using it.

COOKTOP AND TOASTER OVEN OR SLIDE-IN RANGE

An apartment style range with oven (gas or all electric) can be very appealing if you have the room for it. Think about how much baking you actually do. If it is minimal, maybe a toaster oven is all you need. If a cooktop will do, induction burners are my first choice because I think all electric is the easy way to go. If, however, you put in a propane gas system, then you have other options.

APARTMENT SIZE RANGE

At 20" wide these units are the perfect fit for tiny houses. They are available in gas or electric. Unless you are on a permanent location with a hard-wired 100-amp electrical box, you better go with the gas. These almost always come with a kit to convert them to LP gas.

CLOTHES WASHER AND DRYER

All the current rage is a combo washer/dryer in one machine, which has some good features, like 120V, which makes it fit the electric panel better. It is compact, for sure, but the ones I looked at are ventless, which adds moisture to the inside of your home; not a good thing in a tiny space. They also take up to 5 hours to complete a cycle and the sticker shock should scare you off. My preference is an apartment style stacking unit at 26" wide, 27" deep and only 72" high, which still fits under a loft and will only set you back about $1,000. A smaller set at 24" wide for the washer and dryer can also be stacked, albeit they cost as much as a standard width at around $1,000 for each piece!

HEATING, VENTILATION AND AIR CONDITIONING

There are some big decisions to be made here. If you have included a gas system in your home for cooking then of course you will have it available for heating. If only used for cooking, a 5-gallon propane tank might last for several weeks. If you use it for heating as well you could go through a tank in a day or two depending on how cold it is.

With gas available, you could use a gas heater borrowed from the boating world. With a larger THoW you might be able to find a suitable direct-vent gas fireplace. Dickinson brand has a nice selection of these small marine heaters.

Will you need air conditioning? If so, my favorite solution is a Ductless Heat Pump (also called a 'mini-split'). These are available in 120V versions that make it easier to fit within the constraints of your Load Center. You can buy one of these units online and install it yourself, but you should have a professional do the refrigerant-line connections and startup. I have had good luck finding an HVAC person on Craigslist to do this part.

Wood heat is often considered for a THoW. The challenge here is to find a stove that has a small enough output in BTUs that it doesn't literally drive you out of the house to cool off. Most wood stoves also require a certain amount of clearance from combustibles and that can eat up valuable floor space. You'd also need a place to store the wood for at least a day's worth of heating. It can be done, but think through all of the ramifications.

Resources:
Mighty Heat
Cadet Heat
Dickinson

CABINETS & COUNTERTOPS

"Maybe we are all cabinets of wonder."
- Brian Selznick

Now it's time to have some fun and add style to your new home. Nothing sets the tone like the cabinets and countertops. In most tiny homes at least a quarter of the space is used for the kitchen and there are several basic layouts that can work nicely.

GALLEY KITCHEN

Here there are cabinets and appliances on both side walls. This common style gets its name from a boat. If your home is 8'-4" wide on the outside, then it leaves about 7'-7" on the inside from wall to wall. If you put 24" deep cabinets with 25-1/2" countertops, there is 40 inches between the counters to walk through - in essence, a 'one butt' kitchen. Alternatively, there are 18" cabinets readily available with a 19-1/2" countertop. They are usually found in bars and baths and would leave a generous 4'-4" walkway. If you want to use the narrower base cabinets, be sure to plan ahead and order them early. Keep in mind that there are still a lot of small appliances that are 24" deep; even so, they can be placed across from each other so there is only one tight spot to contend with or you could place them at opposite ends of the kitchen.

"L" KITCHEN

This is where one end wall and one side wall are used for the cabinets and appliances. This a great design for tiny homes as it leaves a nice wide work area.

A ONE WALL KITCHEN

This is used most often on longer tiny house models. I like it because of how roomy it makes the width of the home.

CABINETS

Most cabinets you will find today are made with a product called MDF (medium density fiberboard). It is a combination of sawdust and glue that makes a very stable board so it doesn't shrink and swell with the change in humidity in a home. The downside is that the weight is about 100 lbs. per 4' x 8' sheet, so cabinets can quickly put you over your weight limit. It can also be a source of urea formaldehyde. A better choice is plywood and PureBond brand is formaldehyde-free. Cabinets can also be built with 1/2" plywood in place of 3/4" to save on weight.

COUNTERTOPS

Stop and think about your drivers here. The types and styles of countertops are endless. Butcher block is easy to come by and care for, but heavy. Stainless is light, but says 'modern' which might not fit your style. Preformed counters might be easier to install and are available in many materials. Formica on plywood is lightweight and comes in colors and patterns to fit almost any style. Make sure to use a waterbased contact cement if you choose this option.

How are you going to mount your kitchen sink? If it is an undermount than your countertop choice might be different than if it's topmounted or a vessel style that just sits on top.

Another thing to think about is what tools you have to work with to make or build a countertop. That live-edge piece of wood is really cool, but you will need a woodshop and time to cut, glue and finish it. Something is better than the perfect one you can't afford in time or money.

We are getting so close

to move-in day now.

Breathe...

FLOORING

"When you dance, your purpose is not to get to a certain place on the floor. It's to enjoy each step along the way."
- Wayne Dyer

Remember your drivers; this is not the place to get off message or budget. When thinking about flooring, make it easy to clean. You won't have the luxury of extra space, like a mud room, so every time you walk in to your tiny home you'll be bringing in the outside on your shoes.

Simple is good. I like Marmoleum. It's easy to install and biodegradable, so it's 'green.' It lasts a really long time and - my personal favorite - it's easy to sweep and mop up so you can go off to play. Of course there are lots of other options. 3/4" Hardwood flooring can be heavy but at about one pound per square foot, it should not brake the GVW bank. There are also many types of engineered flooring with the advantage of lighter weight and easier installation. One company I like is Ua Floors because of their commitment to health and the environment.There are several ways to attach this type of product so be sure to follow the manufacturers installation instructions.

Tile is very heavy, but if you saved weight in other places you might be able to spend it here and it's better to put the weight down on the floor than up on the roof.

One design trick to defining spaces in a tiny home is to change the flooring style, color and/or material in different areas. With the right design, it can even make spaces look larger. Another advantage to mixing and matching is that you can often find remnants in smaller quantities at bargain prices. If you go this way, be sure to watch out for the thicknesses of the different materials where the edges meet, but know you can usually find a transition piece for just about any floor thickness.

This is a good place to use the take-off sheet in the Bonus Material.

CHAPTER FIFTEEN
Where Can I Live?

Photo courtesy of www.tinydigshotel.com

WHERE CAN I LIVE?

"I'm a very firm believer in karma, and put it this way:
I get a lot of good parking spots."
- Al Jourgensen

LAND USE / ZONING

Okay, this is where the fun and interesting part kicks in. Unfortunately, many land use boards have not caught up with us. You built a Park Model RV so they want to put you in a Park Model park.

That might work if there are any of these near where you want to live; in the Pacific Northwest there aren't any. Okay, now they say you can park it in an RV park. These are also few and far in-between, and often not in the part of town where I would choose to live.

You ask: "What if I have my own land?" Then it depends on how it is zoned. Is it residential? Then probably not. Commercial? You might be able to claim it is a caretaker's temporary residence.

There are some forward-thinking cities and counties. Portland, Oregon recently said they are not going to enforce the 'No, you can't live in an RV here' rule. El Paso County in Colorado has some lenient laws about where you can live in a moveable tiny house. It's happening all across the country. Developers are even turning old RV parks into tiny house communities. New developments are springing up everywhere. Until it happens in your neighborhood, though, you might just need to park and live in it under the radar.

Where I live it is not uncommon to see an RV in someone's back or side yard with an electrical plug and water hooked up to it for months on end. Many jurisdictions technically allow you to use it for only up to 30 days or some other defined period, then you are supposed to tell your 'friend' that they need to leave; times up.

In fact, almost all actions by the local zoning jurisdiction are complaint driven. Translated: if your neighbors don't care, the county probably doesn't either. Make friends with your neighbors. Take them some cookies. Tell them your story. It won't always work, but it does a lot of the time. People don't like to be surprised, and they don't like what they don't know.

You can also be proactive if you have the personality for it. I just emailed my county councilor and invited her over to talk about the moveable tiny house issue. Her office said okay, so I sent them some information ahead of time. I'm expecting a good meeting.

One of the things I have learned from clients it that the farther out of town you are the less people care what you do as long as you don't infringe on their rights.

There really is no reason not to be able to live in your THoW just because someone wants to call it an RV. You are a human and have the right to a clean, dry, warm place to call home.

Resources: **Tiny House Parking** by Ethan Waldman

Now you know what it takes to complete what many in our modern society think is impossible. The building of your own home is an incredible feat. If you choose to embark on this journey, you will know more about what makes a house work than 90% of your friends and neighbors.

To those of you who do take the next step, I wish you well.

To those of you who decide that this is not the right time or the right project for you, that's okay. I do hope you will think about the creative process and apply it in other areas of your life.

Dream | Plan | Make | Enjoy

All Bonus Material and Links are available at
http://artisantinyhouse.com/bonus-material/

Patrick Sughrue built his first tiny house in 1973 on the back of a 1949 Dodge flatbed truck.

He has been involved in the construction industry for over 25 years with an emphasis on green building, energy-efficiency, Net Zero and innovative HVAC.

He and his wife Jill hand-built their own home north of Vancouver, WA with structural insulated panels (SIPs) over 20 years ago.

He has been using SIPs in his designs ever since to help Owner-Builders (DIY) with their moveable tiny homes, Accessory Dwelling Units (ADUs), and small ground-bound cabins, cottages, studios and workshops.

CONTACT US

P: 360.576.6311

E: Office@ArtisanTinyHouse.com

W: ArtisanTinyHouse.com

CPSIA information can be obtained
at www.ICGtesting.com
Printed in the USA
BVHW050511040222
627987BV00001B/8